The AI Service Playbook

Journeys, Guardrails & Economics for Modern Customer Service Operations

by Keith Hamilton & Lionel Thain

The AI Service Playbook

979-8-2955-6565-6 – INGRAM PBK
979-8-2955-8533-3 – INGRAM HC/CL
979-8-2955-6568-7 – INGRAM EBK

ISBN 978-1506-915-75-3 HC/CL
ISBN 978-1506-915-69-2 PBK
ISBN 978-1506-915-70-8 EBK

January 2026

Published and Distributed by
Alliance of Independent Authors in conjunction with
First Edition Design Publishing, Inc.
P.O. Box 17646, Sarasota, FL 34276-3217
www.allianceofindependentauthors.com
www.firsteditiondesignpublishing.com

Disclosure

The use of artificial intelligence carries inherent risks, including but not limited to data privacy concerns, bias, inaccuracies, and unintended outcomes. This book discusses AI strategies and tools for educational purposes only and does not guarantee results.

Readers assume full responsibility for how AI technologies are implemented and used. The author and publisher disclaim any liability arising from the application of the information contained herein.

About The Authors

Keith Hamilton is a UK commercial leader and AI strategist in the contact-centre industry.

keith@absoluteintelligenceuk.com

Lionel Thain is a British entrepreneur whose career has been shaped by data, consumer insight and the mechanics of scalable customer engagement.

lionel@absoluteintelligenceuk.com

They are part of the team that formed Voice Artificial Intelligence in 2025, to combine human expertise and artificial intelligence.

Their focus with this book is to distil all that experience into practical patterns, questions and tools leaders can use to deploy with confidence.

For more about the authors, see page 198.

Introduction

Why read this book?

By the end of this book, you will be able to:

- **Define what 'agentic AI' actually means in customer service, including AI voice 'Agents' and distinguish it from chatbots, analytics and generic automation.**

- **Identify 3–5 high-value use cases in your own operation where AI can change unit economics without increasing risk.**

- **Design blended human–AI journeys including journeys that use AI voice 'Agents' on your phone lines that give customers faster, clearer outcomes while keeping people in control where it matters.**

- **Set practical guardrails and controls that satisfy operational leaders, frontline teams and risk, legal and compliance functions.**

- **Build a business case that boards can sign off, with baselines, benefits, costs and kill switches that survive scrutiny.**

- **Understand how AI and AI voice 'Agents' change the economics of busy, voice-heavy operations without breaking trust or compliance.**

- **Run a 90-day implementation plan that gets from intent selection to live results without promising a "big bang" transformation.**

But first, some context. We're entering a new era in customer service. It is no longer a queue, a headset and a script, it is human teams working alongside AI voice 'Agents' and other assistants built on your data and systems.

Most organisations have spent the last decade reactively squeezing cost, complexity and risk into their contact operations. They would add more channels, more products, more regulation and more reporting, then try to hold it together with heroic agents and an Interactive Voice Response (IVR) that nobody loved.

The result is a pressure cooker of rising expectations, fragile processes and thin margins. teams know the system is creaking but cannot safely change it at speed. When it works, it does so because of individuals, not because the system is well designed. When it fails, the consequences show up in complaints, churn, bad debt, scrutiny and the erosion of trust.

Artificial intelligence arrives in the middle of this muddle, not in a clean lab.

Used well, AI is not a magic brain. It is an infrastructure upgrade. It gives you new ways to handle demand, personalise the process and reduce the effort required from customers and staff.

Used badly, it just adds another layer of risk and noise.

This book is written for leaders who have to live with the consequences of both.

The Pressure Cooker We Built For Ourselves

For years, the answer to growing demand was to add something: another team, another queue, another script variant, another knowledge article, another tech layer. Each new piece made sense locally. Collectively, they produced estates with:

- Fragmented experiences that ask customers to repeat themselves

- Agents who must navigate multiple systems while staying compliant

- Metrics that describe slices of the truth but not the whole picture

- Change processes so slow that workarounds feel like the only option

This is the backdrop against which every AI conversation now happens. If you ignore it, you end up with clever models duct-taped onto broken processes.

If you face it honestly, you have the chance to redesign the work.

Why AI Matters Now

AI improves three properties that govern operations:

1. **Concurrency at low marginal cost.** A well-designed AI system can hold many conversations at once without the same cost curve as hiring and training more people. That does not mean 'replace the contact centre'; it means decoupling panic hiring and overtime from peak demand.

2. **Consistency under policy.** AI does not get tired, bored or distracted. Within the boundaries you set, it will follow the rules every time. In regulated environments that is a particular advantage, as long as the rules are clearly written and enforced in the system rather than scattered across emails and shared drives.

3. **Observability by default.** AI-generated and AI-assisted interactions are inherently text-rich and structured. Done properly, you gain searchable transcripts, intent labels, outcomes and timings for almost every contact. That is a better foundation for improvement than sampling a tiny fraction of voice calls.

AI does not make judgement calls for you. It allows humans to work where judgement, empathy and escalation matter, while AI 'Agents' handle repetitive recognition and retrieval. The question is not 'Will AI replace agents?' but 'How do we redesign service so that each does the work it is best suited to?'

A Practical Stance

Projects fail when teams skip the dull steps that make AI safe and useful:

- **No baselines.** Teams cannot say how many contacts they get for each intent, what current containment looks like or what their cost per resolution really is.
- **No guardrails.** They cannot explain in plain English what the AI is never allowed to do, what must always be escalated and what requires explicit consent.
- **No knowledge discipline.** They feed ungoverned documents into models and then act surprised when the outputs are inconsistent or non-compliant.
- **No reverse gear.** They roll into production without a kill switch, rollback plan or clear pilot exit criteria.

This book takes the opposite approach. It assumes that:

- You will start small, with clearly defined journeys and success measures.
- You will keep humans in the loop where risk or judgement is high.
- You will insist on being able to stop, unwind or re-scope a deployment in days, not months, if it behaves badly or under-delivers.

The method is unglamorous: baselines, playbooks, named owners, documented assumptions, and regular review. It is the only way to turn AI from a series of experiments into part of your operating model.

Why Partner Rather Than Build Alone

You can assemble tools in-house. Most technology teams can spin up models, connect APIs and build proof-of-concepts. The difficulty is not "Can we get something working?" but:

- Can we make it **safe** under current and emerging regulation?
- Can we make it **repeatable** across journeys and business units?
- Can we make it **operationally boring**, so it runs without heroics?

Building that on your own takes time, experimentation and a tolerance for failure that many organisations do not have in the current climate. Partnering with people who have already made the mistakes, set guardrails and built runbooks does not remove your accountability, but it shortens the path to something dependable.

This book does not argue that you should outsource your thinking. It argues that you should be selective about where you build, where you buy and where you partner, so you are not reinventing the wheel in areas where standards already exist.

This is not a data-science textbook or a speculative essay about the far future. It is a field manual for executives, operators and technologists who need to take their existing customer service estate and make it fit for the next decade.

You will see sector examples from utilities, financial services, retail, telecoms, healthcare and more. You will get questions to ask your teams, patterns you can reuse and pitfalls you can avoid. Most importantly, you will get a way to think about AI in customer experience that centres on outcomes, not hype.

The next section looks at how we ended up here: the evolution of customer service, the measures that never went out of fashion, and why attempts to "transform" so often stall. From there, we will build the case for agentic AI that is grounded in operational reality.

Prologue

We've Seen This Film Before

In the late 1990s, the idea that people would buy shoes, holidays, insurance or even groceries over the internet sounded faintly ridiculous to most leaders.

The infrastructure was fragile. Connections were slow. Payment pages timed out. Many customers had never typed their card number into anything other than a chip-and-PIN device in a shop.

If you were running a retailer, a travel firm or a bank, you could tell yourself a comforting story:

"Yes, the internet is interesting. Yes, we should have a website. But our customers like dealing with people. They like branches. They like the phone. They will not trust this new channel with serious money."

For a while, that story was true enough.

Early Adopters V Late Movers

A small minority of organisations made a different bet.

They invested in basic e-commerce when it still looked like a side project. They took the pain of clunky early systems, unreliable modems and warehouse processes that were never designed for single-item picks.

They did three things that, with hindsight, mattered far more than the technology itself:

- They treated digital as part of the core business, not a marketing experiment.

- They built end-to-end journeys, not just brochures, so customers could browse, pay and receive goods without phoning anybody.

- They learned, painfully, how to handle fraud, chargebacks, stockouts, returns and complaints in a world where the customer was not standing in front of them.

For years, the numbers were small. Many boards asked the same question: "Why are we spending scarce capital on something that is still single-digit revenue?"

Then, almost invisibly at first, the curve steepened.

Connection speeds improved. Browsers became more capable. Payment providers got better at handling risk. Customers who had tried one or two online purchases discovered that it was, in fact, simpler than queuing in a branch or sitting on hold.

By the time most people noticed, early adopters had a structural advantage:

- Scale: they could serve national or international demand from centralised operations.

- Convenience: their journeys were open 24/7 and could be completed in minutes, not hours.

- Cost: they could handle many more transactions per staff member than a traditional branch or call centre estate.

Late movers tried to catch up. Some did. Many did not. We remember the names that disappeared, but there are far more companies that survived with permanently higher costs, weaker customer loyalty and limited room to invest.

They did not fail because the internet 'didn't work'. They failed because they treated an infrastructure shift as a marginal channel decision for too long.

The Same Pattern, Different Technology

Today, conversational AI is going through the same pattern.

Most organisations have experimented with chatbots, FAQs and simple automation. Many have also tried small pilots with large language models. A few have already put AI into serious production.

The same comforting stories are circulating in boardrooms:

- "Our customers will never trust an AI with sensitive issues."
- "We are in a regulated sector; the risk is too high."
- "We already have a contact centre. We just need more people, better training and better scripts."

At the same time, a smaller group of organisations are making a different choice.

They are not treating AI as a novelty, a lab experiment or a single channel. They are treating it as the next infrastructure layer for service:

- They are redesigning journeys so that routine, rule-based work is handled by 'Agents' that can operate concurrently, consistently and observably across channels.
- They are building one rulebook and one set of golden answers that humans and AI both use, rather than letting knowledge scatter across inboxes and PDFs.
- They are putting guardrails, logging, identity checks and kill switches in place so that they can move quickly without losing control of risk.

The technology itself is still evolving. Some models will improve; some platforms will disappear. That is not the main question for leaders.

The main question is whether you treat this shift as:

- a new channel to be bolted on to an already strained estate, or
- a chance to re-architect how workflows, who does what, and how you balance cost, risk and customer effort.

The difference will not be obvious in month one. It will be decisive over three to five years.

What Changes, What Stays the Same

There are obvious differences between the early internet and today's agentic AI.

The internet was primarily about distribution and access: how customers found you and how you got products and services to them. Agentic AI is primarily about how work flows inside your operation: who handles which decisions, with what information, under what guardrails.

But many of the underlying dynamics are the same:

- Trust is earned, not assumed. Customers will trust AI when it reliably solves real problems and escalates smoothly when needed, not because you tell them to.
- Early competence compounds. Teams that learn how to deploy AI safely and economically now will be better placed to adopt future capabilities.
- Delay is not neutral. Waiting "until things settle" often means adopting under pressure, with less choice, weaker negotiating power and more operational pain.

In other words, we have seen this film before.

How To Read the Rest of This Book

This book is not about chasing every new model or tool. It is about building the operational, ethical and economic foundations that will let you:

- move faster than your competitors,
- stay inside your risk appetite, and
- avoid another decade of fragmented channels, reactive fire-fighting and rising downstream costs.

In the chapters that follow, we will:

- define what we mean by agentic AI in customer service, and how it differs from generic chatbots,
- show you the cross-sector patterns that repeat in utilities, financial services, telecoms, retail and other service-heavy sectors,
- walk through how to redesign end-to-end journeys with clear boundaries between human, AI and core systems,
- set out the guardrails, legal duties and ethical principles that must be baked in from day one,
- and give you a business case and optimisation playbook that a board can actually approve and govern.

You do not have to become a machine-learning expert to act on any of this.

You do, however, have to take seriously the idea that conversational AI, including AI voice 'Agents' on your phone lines, is becoming a primary layer for how customers interact with you and how work is done.

The organisations that understand this early will not simply "handle more calls with fewer people." They will change the shape of their operations.

Those who wait will still end up deploying AI. They will just do it later, with less control, under more pressure, and on terms set by others.

We have seen this film before. The question is which role you want to play in the sequel?

Chapter 1

The Evolution of Customer Service and AI Voice Agents

In this Chapter we show how customer service evolved from manual, voice-only call centres and IVR menus to today's blended operations with AI and AI voice 'Agents'.

From switchboards to something almost sensible

Customer service started as a routing problem.

A customer called a number. A human on a switchboard listened, recognised roughly what the caller wanted and plugged them through to someone who might be able to help. Most of the work was manual: listening, remembering, deciding and connecting.

The constraints were obvious:

- Not enough opening hours.
- Not enough lines.
- Not enough people who knew enough to act.

The experience was slow, inconsistent and often dependent on the mood and memory of whoever answered. Yet it was also personal, and customers were oddly forgiving. Expectations were lower, choices were fewer and both sides accepted the limits.

Then organisations industrialised the process.

Interactive voice response (IVR) systems tried to turn routing into a machine problem: "Press 1 for billing, 2 for technical support." The intention was rational enough: handle more calls, direct them to the right team and reduce the strain on operators.

In practice, many customers experienced IVR as a locked gate, rather than a guide. Menus grew longer, wording became more defensive, and "I'm sorry, I didn't quite catch that" became a familiar irritant. The goal of efficient routing collided with the reality of messy, multi-topic, impatient human queries.

Still, the direction of travel was set: away from one-to-one conversations and towards scaled operations.

The forces that shaped the modern contact centre

Before anyone said 'AI' three pressures reshaped customer operations.

1. **Volume and volatility of demand** Contact volumes grew with product complexity, digital self-service and marketing reach. Peaks became sharper: billing cycles, outages, sales promotions, strikes, weather events and media stories all landed on the same queues.

2. **Channel proliferation** Voice was joined by email, web forms, live chat, messaging apps and social media. Each new channel arrived with the promise of 'deflecting' volume but often ended up adding more touchpoints for the same underlying problems.

3. **Cost and compliance pressure** Regulators tightened rules; boards tightened budgets. Operations leaders had to handle more contacts, at higher quality and with more compliance, with less flex to simply add headcount.

The net effect was a system constrained by **human concurrency**, **human memory** and **human inconsistency at peak**. You could not realistically train every agent on every scenario or guarantee perfect compliance under pressure.

Most organisations responded by adding more layers: more teams, more queues, more scripts, more SLAs (service level agreements), more reports. The work got done, but often in spite of the system, not because of it.

Knowledge as a product, not a wish

Things began to improve when leaders started treating knowledge as a product instead of a vague aspiration.

The early idea was simple:

- Put the right answers in a knowledge base.
- Train agents to search and follow them.

The reality was messier: stale articles, duplicate versions, unclear ownership and documents written in language customers would never use. A perfectly accurate policy hidden in a shared drive did nothing for the employee on the phone trying to work out whether a fee could be waived.

The turning point came when organisations applied product discipline to knowledge:

- **Defined owners and review cycles** for critical content.
- **Versioning and change logs** so people knew what had changed and why.
- **Plain-language patterns** that matched real customer phrases instead of internal jargon.

Good knowledge reduced the cognitive load on agents and shortened calls. Bad knowledge increased handle time, repeat contact and escalation. The difference was not the software; it was ownership and discipline.

Orchestration: from reading to doing

Knowledge alone still left gaps. An agent might find the right article, but the actual work was spread across systems: CRM, billing, fulfilment, identity checks, notes, email. The agent had to stitch it all together in real time.

Cloud platforms and APIs (application programming interfaces) changed what was possible. Instead of every agent manually:

- Looking up the account.
- Checking status in multiple systems.
- Applying rules.
- Triggering actions and recording outcomes.

Orchestrated flows could be designed, bundling those steps into a single pathway. The job shifted from "agent remembers sequence and clicks everywhere" to "agent follows a guided flow that handles the plumbing."

This did not remove human judgement, but it **reduced the random factor**. Two agents following the same flow were more likely to produce consistent outcomes. It also created a foundation for automation: once a flow is codified and observable, you can start to ask which parts really require a human.

Why artificial intelligence is the logical next step

Artificial intelligence arrives at estates that already have routing, knowledge and orchestration in some form. It is not the first wave of change; it is the next.

AI matters because it improves three operational properties that have constrained service for decades:

1. **Concurrency at low marginal cost** A well-designed AI system can handle many contacts at once without the

same linear cost curve as human staffing. This does not mean you remove people. It means you decouple peak demand from frantic hiring, agency usage and overtime.

2. **Consistency under policy** Once you translate rules into prompts, policies and guardrails, AI applies them the same way every time. It does not skip a step because the queue is long or the previous call was stressful. This is especially valuable in regulated sectors, provided the rules are clear and maintained.

3. **Observability by default** AI-assisted and AI-handled interactions produce structured, searchable records by design: transcripts, intents, actions, outcomes and timings. That provides a better basis for improvement than listening to a small sample of calls and guessing the rest.

In combination, these properties let you design service differently:

- Routine recognition and retrieval can be moved to machines.

- Human time can be concentrated where context, judgement and relationship matter.

- Change can be deployed and measured in days and weeks instead of quarters and years.

AI is not a disembodied intelligence hovering above your estate. It is another way to route, decide and act. Its real impact depends on how you connect it to the journeys, systems and people you already have.

The measures that never went out of fashion

New technology arrives with new jargon. The fundamentals of performance have not changed.

The same core measures apply whether work is done by people, AI or both:

Measure	What it actually tells you
Containment	Whether the interaction was fully resolved in-channel without creating extra work elsewhere
Average handle time (AHT)	How long it really takes to resolve, including talk, wrap, transfers and queued work
First-contact resolution (FCR)	How often you solve the problem first time, from the customer's perspective
Customer satisfaction (CSAT)	How customers feel about the experience, not just the outcome
Cost per resolution (CPR)	What it costs to fully resolve an interaction, including rework and overhead
Value per resolution (VPR)	The financial value created or protected per resolved interaction (revenue, debt recovered, churn avoided)
Latency and its percentiles	How long customers actually wait, and what the slowest 5–10% experience

The temptation with AI is to chase only the metrics that make the slideware look good: 'containment above 80%', 'average handle time cut in half', 'CSAT uplift by x points'.

Those numbers matter. They are also easy to game or misread. A bot that ends the conversation quickly without solving the problem will appear to have excellent AHT and containment until you factor in:

- Repeat contacts.
- Escalations.
- Complaints.
- Downstream costs.

The point of using these measures is not to win a leaderboard. It is to **govern reality**: to see whether your changes are making life better or worse for customers, staff and the P&L (profit and loss account).

Dashboards that do not influence a decision next week are decoration. The useful ones are small, stable and attached to specific owners.

Why attempts still fail (and how to stop repeating it)

Most stalled 'transformation' projects may appear to rhyme (the stories are not identical, but they sound very similar) but the technology changes; the failure patterns do not.

Common patterns include:

- **Hype-led scope.** Setting out to 'transform the contact centre' rather than fixing a small number of journeys thoroughly.
- **No credible baseline.** Not knowing current intent volumes, containment, AHT or CPR, which makes every claimed benefit speculative.
- **Copying surface features.** Recreating a competitor's chatbot or voice bot without understanding their estate, constraints or failure modes.
- **Ignoring failure handling.** Designing the 'happy path' only, with no serious thought about what happens when the AI is unsure, wrong or blocked.
- **Thin governance.** No single, plain-English rulebook for what the AI is allowed to say and do; no agreed kill switch; no schedule for review.

The antidote is unglamorous and effective:

- **One rulebook of guardrails**, written in plain English, covering disclosure, identity, vulnerable customers, red lines, payment by verified link, language limits and rollback rules.

- **Trustworthy knowledge** with named owners, version history and review dates, with locked 'golden answers' where regulation cares.

- **Observable outcomes at intent level**, with a simple error taxonomy (a dozen categories is enough) and named owners to fix causes, not just symptoms.

- **Respectful handoffs** that feel like a continuation, not a rescue, with clear signalling of what has already been attempted and what comes next.

None of this requires a moonshot. It requires adults, a calendar and the will to retire one error class at a time.

What actually changed for people

For customers, the promise of AI is not novelty. It is fewer hoops, less repetition and faster, clearer outcomes.

For frontline staff, the promise is less time spent on:

- Repeating identity checks.
- Looking up the same policy for the hundredth time.
- Copying notes between systems.
- Apologising for processes they do not control.

And more time spent on:

- Handling complex, sensitive or high-value situations.
- Sorting out edge cases the system was not designed for.
- Feeding back where processes and policies are broken.

That requires conscious design. If you deploy AI simply to absorb volume without redesigning journeys and roles, you risk creating a two-tier experience: automated frustration up front, and humans left with only the hardest, most emotionally draining work.

If, instead, you design AI and human roles together, you can improve both the **customer experience** and the **agent experience**.

How this sets up the rest of the book

Everything that follows builds on a simple theme:

Customer service evolved through routing, knowledge and orchestration; AI is the next layer, not a parallel universe.

The implications are practical:

- You will not be starting from scratch; you will be reshaping what already exists.
- The same measures that govern human operations will govern AI-enabled ones.
- The constraints that made earlier attempts fail are still present; you cannot ignore them.

The next three chapters take this foundation and apply it:

- **Chapter 2** defines agentic AI in concrete terms and distinguishes it from generic automation, including what makes AI voice 'Agents' different from yesterday's IVR scripts.
- **Chapter 3** identifies cross-sector patterns and boundaries so you can see where AI and AI voice 'Agents' are naturally suited and where they are not.

- **Chapter 4** zooms in on customer journeys and shows how to redesign them so humans, AI and AI voice 'Agents' each doing the work they are best at.

By the time you return to your own estate, you should be able to trace any proposed AI project back to the basics in this chapter: routing, knowledge, orchestration, measures and guardrails.

A note on partnering with specialists

You can assemble components internally: models, orchestration tools, telephony, analytics. Many teams already have prototypes running in labs and sandboxes.

The harder task is to:

- Make those prototypes **safe** enough for real customers.
- Make them **repeatable** across journeys and business units.
- Make them **operationally boring**: predictable, observable and recoverable when something goes wrong.

Specialists who live in this space every day bring two forms of leverage:

- **Pattern leverage:** lessons from multiple deployments in different sectors, including the mistakes.
- **Operational leverage:** runbooks, playbooks, guardrails and reporting that have already been battle-tested.

Partnering does not remove your accountability. It shortens the distance between where you are and a state where AI is embedded in your operating model, not trialled as an interesting experiment.

That is the context in which this book is written: not AI as a spectacle, but AI as the next step in a long, very human attempt to serve customers at scale without losing control.

Chapter 2

Understanding agentic AI and AI voice agents in customer service

In this Chapter we define what we mean by 'agentic' in customer service, and we keep tying that definition back to how AI voice 'Agents' should behave when they are the ones talking to your customers.

Key frameworks:

- *The 7-move agentic loop:*

Listen, Plan, Retrieve, Act (via tools), Check the world changed, Summarise, decide to close or escalate.

- *The 7-part architecture:*

Channels, Journeys, Knowledge, 'Agents', Tools & integrations, Observability, Governance.

- *Planning discipline:*

Plan the smallest safe next step; treat each move as a constrained decision.

- *Identity, consent, lawful basis:*

Lawful basis, disclosure, escalation paths for anything sensitive.

- *Knowledge as software:*

Versioned, tested, owned, retired.

- *Tools and write-paths:*

Whitelisted actions, explicit write access, no mystery side-effects.

- *Handoffs that feel like 'continue':*

Summary packets, next best actions, preserved context.

- *Economics in one line:*

Cost per resolution (CPR) and capacity framing for agentic versus human.

- *Capacity and concurrency:*

Thinking properly about peaks and staffing.

- *Testing, rollout, change:*

Pilot, guardrails, change control, avoid cowboy releases.

2.1 Plain-English definition

'Agentic' means the assistant can plan and take the next safe step on its own, within boundaries you set.

It is not a static FAQ, a scripted chatbot or a single API call. It is a small decision-maker that can:

- Understand what the customer is trying to achieve.
- Decide which tools to use.
- Apply your policies.
- Act, check and adjust.

It operates inside a rulebook, because it is incapable of independent action. Which means that it will never freelance outside those rules, never invent outcomes and never pretend that a half-answer is a resolution.

The loop at the heart of this book is seven moves long:

1. **Listen** to understand the customer's goal and constraints.
2. **Plan** the smallest safe step that advances that goal.
3. **Retrieve** the policy or knowledge needed to act correctly.
4. **Act** via whitelisted tools that read or write in systems of record.
5. **Check** that the world actually changed as intended.
6. **Summarise** what changed and what happens next, in plain English.
7. **Decide** whether to close or escalate with a concise handoff packet.

Everything else – prompts, routing, logging, reporting, controls – exists so this loop runs predictably, safely and quickly.

Keep this picture in mind. If a proposed 'AI solution' does not clearly implement this loop, with your rules and your tools, it is not agentic in the sense this book uses the word.

2.2 Architecture you can explain to a board

An agentic service has seven moving parts. Each is deliberately boring.

1. **Channels**
   Voice, chat, email, forms and messaging carry words. They do not make decisions. They take input, deliver output and provide basic metadata (who, when, where).

2. **Guardrails**
   The rulebook:

   - Disclosure, identity and verification steps.
   - Lawful basis and consent where required.
   - 'Do not automate' zones (e.g. certain complaints, complex vulnerability cases).
   - Rules for payment, collections and vulnerable customers.
   - Language limits and escalation triggers.

Guardrails are written in plain English, agreed with risk, legal and compliance, then encoded into prompts, policies and code.

3. **Orchestrator**
   The small 'brain' that runs the seven-step loop. It:

   - Turns raw text into a goal, constraints and context.
   - Builds a short plan (one to three steps).
   - Calls tools, applies guardrails and re-plans as the world changes.

Its job is not to be clever. Its job is to be predictable, observable and reversible.

4. **Knowledge**
   Owned, versioned answers with review dates. Regulated wording is locked as **golden answers**. The assistant is 100% dependent on the knowledge, unable to treat it as , a suggestion.

5. **Tools**
   Whitelisted, named actions that talk to systems of record:

   - get balance(customer_id)

- create_payment_link(customer_id, amount, purpose)
- update_contact(customer_id, address)
- reserve_slot(order_id, slot_id)
- raise_ticket(customer_id, category, summary)

Each tool has clear inputs, outputs, validation and post-conditions. If a tool does not exist, the 'Agent' does not promise that outcome.

6. **Observability** Four lenses:

- **Experience:** intents, containment, FCR, CSAT, latency percentiles.
- **Economics:** AHT, CPR, VPR, cost split between human and AI.
- **Quality & safety:** error types, escalations, compliance breaches avoided or triggered.
- **Change:** versions of prompts, tools and knowledge in play during each interaction.

7. **Security**
Least privilege for tools; SSO (single sign-on) / MFA (multi-factor authentication) for consoles; encryption; change control with reverse gear; audit trails that stand up to regulators and internal audit.

If you can sketch this on a slide and label where you are strong, weak or missing, you are ahead of most organisations. The point is not the terminology. The point is to stop treating 'AI' as a single opaque box and start treating it as an architecture you can govern.

2.3 Why conversational AI assistants behave differently from generic chatbots

When most people think about AI in service, they think about the public chatbots they have tried on websites or apps.

Those systems are usually powered by a general-purpose large language model (LLM). You type a question; the model predicts a plausible answer based on patterns in its training data. It does not know your customer, your policies or your systems. It is not connected to your records.

That design is powerful for open-ended questions. It is also why those systems can appear to hallucinate, generating confident answers that are not grounded in your data or rules.

In this book, we are interested in a different pattern: conversational service assistants that operate inside your estate, under your governance, using your systems of record.

Two very different designs

A generic chatbot is usually:

- connected to the public internet or a broad knowledge base,
- free to answer almost any question in natural language,
- not constrained by your specific policies, journeys or data.

A service assistant built on an agentic architecture is different; it is:

- scoped to specific journeys and purposes - for example, 'help customers understand and manage their water bill'

- grounded in a controlled knowledge base - your approved policies, FAQs and process guides,

- integrated with internal systems via whitelisted tools - for example, 'get bill', 'take a reading', 'set up a payment plan'

- governed by a rulebook that sets out what it can and cannot do.

The underlying model might still be a large language model. The behaviour changes because of what you allow it to access, how you constrain its actions and how you monitor it.

How enterprise assistants get their answers

When a service assistant answers a question, it typically follows the pattern introduced earlier in this chapter:

- listen to the customer

- plan the next safe step under the current rulebook

- retrieve information from a verified source (for example, your billing platform or an approved knowledge article)

- act via a tool or integration, if something in the real world needs to change

- check that the world has changed as expected

- summarise what has happened in language the customer can understand

- decide whether to close the interaction or escalate to a human

The critical point is that the information step and the action step are constrained calls to your own systems and content.

The assistant does not invent a balance. It calls a billing API.

It does not make up eligibility criteria. It retrieves the policy article you have approved.

If it cannot find what it needs, it should follow a designed fallback path - for example, offering to connect the customer to a person with the right access.

What this means for accuracy and risk

This design does not make the assistant perfect. It does change the risk profile compared with a generic chatbot.

Done properly, a conversational service assistant:

- reduces the risk of fabrication by relying on systems of record and curated knowledge rather than open internet search
- reduces inconsistency by using the same rulebook and golden answers as your human agents
- makes errors more observable by logging every tool call, every prompt and every response for review
- keeps you closer to your risk appetite by enforcing boundaries on what the assistant may say and do

Things can still go wrong

Your systems of record can contain outdated or incorrect data. Integrations can fail or return incomplete information. The assistant can be misconfigured or deployed into scenarios you did not design it for.

That is why the guardrails in this book - identity checks, disclosure, escalation paths, logging, monitoring, incident response and kill switches - are not optional extras. They are part of the architecture.

The point is not that 'our assistant never hallucinates'. The point is that you design the assistant so that it has far fewer opportunities to fabricate, and give it clear routes to escalate when it is unsure.

Why this matters for leaders

For leaders, this distinction matters because it changes the questions you ask.

Instead of 'Can we trust AI in customer service?', the question becomes: 'Under what scope, data, rulebook and guardrails are we willing to let an assistant act?'

Instead of 'Will the model hallucinate?', the question becomes: 'How have we designed the assistant to minimise fabrication, detect issues quickly and recover safely when something goes wrong?'

Instead of treating all AI as the same risk, you can have a more precise conversation about journeys, boundaries and controls.

Generic chatbots and public LLM interfaces will continue to be useful for exploration, drafting and internal productivity. They are not the pattern you should copy for regulated, high-stakes or emotionally charged customer work.

The rest of this book assumes you are interested in the service assistant pattern: conversational 'Agents' that operate inside your organisation, on your data, under your guardrails.

2.4 The planning discipline

Planning is intentionally short.

The orchestrator never creates a long, fragile plan. It:

- Builds a **micro-plan** of at most three steps.
- Executes step one.

- Checks what happened.
- Re-plans as needed.

A typical micro-plan template looks like this:

1. Confirm identity to the required level for the requested action.
2. Retrieve the minimum data needed to act (policy, account, status).
3. Attempt a single change with a known tool, then check and summarise.

This discipline has three benefits:

- **Fewer cascading errors.** If a step fails, you see it quickly and can recover.
- **Easier reasoning.** Humans can understand what the 'Agent' was trying to do and why.
- **Safer change.** When you change tools or policies, the blast radius is smaller.

When you hear teams talk about 'plans' in an agentic system, they should be able to show you these small, checkable plans, not 15-step fantasies.

2.5 Identity, consent and lawful basis

Most serious failures involve identity and lawful basis. Get these wrong and nothing else matters.

The 'Agent' must be able to answer, for every interaction:

Who are we speaking to?

- Identity level (e.g. unverified, partially verified, fully verified).
- Method used (e.g. password, OTP, documents checked by a human).

What are we allowed to do?

- Lawful basis (e.g. contract, legal obligation, legitimate interests, consent).
- Channel-specific constraints (e.g. no disclosure of sensitive data in certain channels).

What have we told the customer?

- Disclosure that they are speaking to an AI assistant.
- What data is being used, for what, and how they can opt out where applicable.

These rules belong in the guardrail book and the orchestration logic, not in scattered emails and training slides. They must be testable. You should be able to ask:

- 'Show me ten random contacts where we set up a payment plan for a new customer last week,' and see the identity, lawful basis and disclosures used.

If the system cannot provide that evidence, it is not ready for scale.

2.6 Knowledge that behaves like software

Most AI failures are knowledge failures in disguise.

To avoid that, treat knowledge like software:

- **Owners.** Every topic has a named owner with an inbox and a calendar.
- **Versions and reviews.** Answers have version numbers and next-review dates.
- **Golden answers.** Regulated or risk-bearing statements are locked, cited and reused verbatim.
- **Reading age and tone.** Plain, neutral, concrete language. No theatrics.
- **Citations.** Internal responses record which version was used, so differences in outcome can be traced to content changes, not to 'AI behaviour'.

The assistant should:

- Prefer golden answers where they exist.
- Defer or escalate when no answer meets the policy standard.
- Avoid 'hallucinating' by design, through retrieval constraints and prompts that favour saying 'I don't know' over guessing.

Honesty is faster than confident nonsense. Customers forgive clear limits; regulators do not forgive creative improvisation.

2.7 Tools and write-paths

Resolution requires write-paths. Reading data is not enough.

A **tool** is a small, named capability with:

- Validated inputs (types, ranges, required fields).

- Defined outputs (including failure states).
- Post-conditions that describe what the world should look like after success.

Examples:

- get_balance(customer_id) → **returns currency, amount, timestamp.**
- create_payment_link(customer_id, amount, purpose) → **returns URL, expiry, state.**
- update_contact(customer_id, address) → **returns success flag and new state.**
- reserve_slot(order_id, slot_id) → **returns confirmation code.**
- raise_ticket(customer_id, category, summary) → **returns ticket_id and owner.**

Every tool is whitelisted. The 'Agent' cannot call arbitrary systems; it can only use these defined paths.

Design principles:

- **Narrow and composable.** Many small tools beat a few giant ones.
- **Idempotent where possible.** Safe to retry if the assistant is unsure whether a step succeeded.
- **Safe failure modes.** Failing closed with a clear error is better than partial, silent success.

If a write-path does not exist, the 'Agent' must not promise that outcome. It should explain the limit and either offer what is possible or escalate to a human who has a different set of tools.

2.8 Handoffs that feel like 'continue'

Escalation is normal. The goal is to make it feel like progress, not failure.

From the customer's perspective, escalation should sound like:

"I'll bring a colleague in. They'll see everything we've done so far."

From the advisor's perspective, a good handoff packet includes:

- Identity status and method.
- The customer's stated goal, in their own words.
- Steps attempted so far, with outcomes.
- Relevant artefacts (files, photos, forms).
- System state that matters (balances, flags, tickets raised).
- Suggested next actions, clearly marked as suggestions.

Advisors should open with a two-sentence restart that acknowledges the work done:

> *"I can see you spoke with our assistant about setting up a payment plan. They've already confirmed your details and created a summary of your options. Let's go through them together."*

When you do this, three things happen:

- Repeats fall.
- AHT on escalated contacts falls.
- Complaint risk falls, because customers feel carried, not dropped.

The 'Agent' is not a gate. It is the front part of a joined-up journey.

2.9 Economics in one line

Economics must survive a whiteboard.

At its simplest:

CPR (Cost per Resolution) = total handling minutes × unit cost across the **entire path** (AI + human + waiting).

The steepest lever is reducing human minutes on common tasks while holding quality.

You should always show ±10% sensitivity on:

- Containment rate.
- Escalated minutes per resolution.

Ranges are more honest than spurious precision. A typical blended line might look like:

- 70–80% of intents fully contained by AI at negligible marginal cost.
- 20–30% escalated with lower AHT because identity, context and options are pre-built.
- Overall CPR down, CSAT up or flat, complaint volumes stable or falling.

If a proposed AI deployment looks good only with optimistic containment and no allowance for rework, you have a forecast, not a business case.

2.10 Capacity and concurrency in practice

Concurrency is the quiet force.

By absorbing high-frequency, low-complexity work, an assistant:

- Flattens peaks that would otherwise trigger overtime, agency use or service failure.
- Releases human minutes for judgement-heavy work.
- Allows more slots for outbound work that protects revenue or prevents problems.

Prove it with data, not slogans. Show:

- p95 and p99 latency before and after, not just averages.
- Queue depth at the top three spikes in a typical week.
- Human minutes per resolution on scoped intents trending down.
- Occupancy smoothed without heroic overtime or 'all hands on deck' days.

This is how you argue that capacity has been released without promising unrealistic headcount cuts.

2.11 Testing, rollout and change

Change should feel routine, not dramatic.

Agentic systems live or die on how you handle day-to-day change:

- **Feature flags per intent.** Turn journeys on or off without touching everything else.
- **Dark launches.** Exercise paths end-to-end without visible effects, to catch integration issues.
- **Canary traffic.** Start with a small, controlled fraction of volume and watch metrics before scaling.

- **Release windows.** Avoid launching major changes into known peak periods or crisis conditions.

- **Reverse gear.** Rollback plans that can be executed in minutes if something behaves badly.

Your change log should let you answer:

- 'What changed?'
- 'When?'
- 'For whom?'
- 'How did it affect containment, CPR, CSAT and complaint volumes?'

If you cannot connect those dots, you are not in control; the system is.

Takeaway. Agentic AI is not cleverness for its own sake. It is **a small, safe loop** running inside fences, supported by owned knowledge and simple arithmetic, with people in the right places. Get the loop, the fences and the measures right, and you will resolve more, escalate better, and spend less time explaining why something went wrong.

Chapter 3

Sector-agnostic patterns and boundaries for AI and AI voice agents

The aim of this Chapter is to help leaders think in patterns instead of sectors.

Core frameworks:

Patterns over sectors: move from 'utilities vs telco' to 'identity vs payments vs complaints and other recurring problem types.

Four recurring patterns:

1) Identity and access.

2) Data and preference change.

3) Money in and out.

4) Complaints, risk and vulnerability.

RAG boundary model:

- *Green – fully automatable.*
- *Amber – AI assists or proposes; human confirms.*
- *Red – human-led, AI support only.*

- *Cross-sector examples: showing these patterns in utilities, financial services, and others.*
- *Work that remains human-led: high judgement, high stakes, vulnerability, novel scenarios.*
- *Designing boundaries in practice: convert RAG thinking into concrete rules and workflows.*

3.1 Why patterns matter more than sectors

Most organisations like to think their sector is unique.

The language differs, the regulators differ and the acronyms are lovingly home-grown. Underneath that, the work that lands in customer operations is remarkably similar.

Across utilities, financial services, retail, telecoms, healthcare, travel and insurance, the same patterns repeat:

- Proving who someone is.
- Looking things up.
- Changing details.
- Taking or making payments.
- Explaining decisions.
- Handling complaints and vulnerability.

If you focus on these patterns instead of sector labels, you can:

- Reuse designs and guardrails from one domain in another.
- Build fewer, stronger templates instead of a new approach for each team.

- Avoid arguing about whether "our sector is too special for AI" and focus on where it is actually safe and useful.

This chapter lays out common patterns and a simple way to decide what AI should and should not do.

3.2 Four recurring patterns

Across sectors, four patterns dominate AI conversations in service:

1. **Identity & access**
2. **Data & preference change**
3. **Money in and out**
4. **Complaints, risk and vulnerability**

Each pattern cuts across channels and products. Each has its own natural limits for automation.

3.2.1 Identity & access

Identity work shows up whenever a customer wants to see, change or authorise something that affects them.

Examples:

- Logging in, recovering access, resetting security details.
- Confirming identity before disclosing account or case information.
- Adding or removing authority on an account.

AI is well-suited to:

- Explaining what information is needed and why.

- Guiding customers through steps (e.g. sending and verifying one-time passcodes, checking known facts).
- Coordinating checks across multiple systems and summarising the result.

AI should not:

- Invent shortcuts because a customer is frustrated.
- Bypass required checks to hit a handle-time target.
- Decide to accept "near enough" matches when rules require exact ones.

Identity rules must be set centrally and tested. If your assistant is improvising identity policy, you do not have an assistant; you have a liability.

3.2.2 Data & preference change

Once identity is established, many contacts boil down to "change something in the record":

- Updating address, contact details or communication preferences.
- Adding, removing or updating products and services where eligibility rules are straightforward.
- Capturing missing information needed to progress a case or order.

AI is naturally strong where:

- The rules for change are clear and bounded (e.g. "we can change this detail if X and Y are true").

- The write-paths are well-defined tools, not fragile backdoors.
- There is a clear post-condition (e.g. “address updated” plus confirmation).

Boundaries matter where:

- Changes have legal or long-term financial consequences.
- Changes can only be reversed with difficulty or loss.
- A wrong change would create immediate harm.

In those cases, AI can prepare and confirm data, but a human should approve before final commit.

3.2.3 Money in and out

Money changes the tone of everything.

Patterns:

- Taking payments and setting up instalment plans.
- Issuing refunds, credits or compensation.
- Managing arrears, collections and forbearance.

AI works well when:

- It never handles card details or raw payment data and uses **verified links** and trusted payment providers instead.
- It follows clear rules on what plans or offers are available and does not invent its own.

- It can calculate options, explain trade-offs and generate compliant summaries for the customer to accept.

AI should not:

- Make discretionary forbearance decisions outside policy.
- Threaten or harass customers to recover money.
- Override affordability, vulnerability or regulatory rules in pursuit of collection.

The safest pattern is: **AI structures the discussion, presents compliant options and initiates a secure process**; humans set policy, handle edge cases and review exceptions.

3.2.4 Complaints, risk and vulnerability

Complaints and vulnerability are where organisations most often get into public trouble.

Patterns:

- Formal complaints, including regulated timelines and stages.
- Disputes over decisions, charges, denials or service quality.
- Contacts from or about customers in vulnerable circumstances.

AI can help by:

- Capturing the story in the customer's own words.
- Clarifying what outcome the customer is seeking.

- Explaining processes and timelines in plain language.
- Drafting case summaries for complaint handlers.

AI should not:

- Decide complaint outcomes where those outcomes carry legal, regulatory or life-changing weight.
- Argue with or emotionally pressure vulnerable customers.
- Close complaints or risk cases without human review.

In these journeys, the assistant is primarily a **triage and translation layer**, not the decision-maker.

3.3 A simple Red / Amber / Green boundary

You do not need a complex taxonomy to govern AI. You need a rule that a bored advisor can remember.

A useful starting point:

Zone	What AI can do	What humans must retain
Green	Decide and act within policy.	Set the policy and review performance.
Amber	Propose an action or decision, then ask for approval.	Approve, decline or amend; own the final decision.
Red	Provide information and gather detail; no decisions.	Decide, commit and explain; own outcomes and accountability.

You can then classify work items by zone.

Typical **Green** examples:

- Balance queries, order status, simple FAQs.
- Address and contact detail changes with clear validation.
- Appointment bookings and rebookings.
- Basic product changes where eligibility rules are simple and codified.

Typical **Amber** examples:

- Payment plans within a defined range of options.
- Routine refunds or credits below a threshold.
- Low-risk data changes that affect service but not rights or ownership.

Typical **Red** examples:

- Complaints and appeals with regulatory weight.
- Complex vulnerability handling and safeguarding.
- Terminations, evictions, repossessions, declines of critical services.
- Large financial decisions or forbearance outside standard policy.

For each journey, you can ask:

- Which steps are clearly Green?
- Which are clearly Red?
- Where is there a genuine Amber middle ground?

If your map shows everything as Green, you are being reckless. If it shows everything as Red, you are wasting potential. The right answer is a layered one.

3.4 Cross-sector examples

To make this concrete, consider how the same pattern looks in different sectors.

Utilities: missed payment

Green:

- Explain the bill, due date and consequences of non-payment.
- Confirm identity and read current balance and usage.
- Offer standardised repayment options within policy.
- Generate and send a secure payment link.

Amber:

- Propose a payment plan at the edge of policy, with clear pros and cons.
- Flag indicators of potential vulnerability for human review.

Red:

- Decide on supply disconnection or enforcement action.
- Agree bespoke forbearance or write-off outside standard options.

Retail: late delivery and refund

Green:

- Track order, identify delay, and explain updated delivery estimate.
- Apply standard "late delivery" policy (e.g. refund shipping, issue voucher).
- Process simple returns and refunds within clear thresholds via secure tools.

Amber:

- Propose a goodwill gesture just above standard, based on customer history.

Red:

- Resolve alleged fraud, high-value claims, or serial abuse of policies.

Financial services: card charge dispute

Green:

- Gather details about the disputed transaction.
- Explain dispute process and timelines.
- Submit a properly structured dispute case.

Amber:

- Propose next steps based on clear rules (e.g. temporary credit where allowed).

Red:

- Decide liability in complex disputes.
- Close disputes with major financial consequences.

Healthcare: appointment and records

Green:

- Book, reschedule or cancel routine appointments.
- Provide general, non-diagnostic information and administrative guidance.

Amber:

- Suggest suitable appointment types based on symptoms, within locally agreed protocols.

Red:

- Provide diagnoses, medication decisions or triage in high-risk cases.
- Change clinical records without professional oversight.

Telecoms: package change and complaint

Green:

- Explain current plan, usage and standard upgrade options.
- Apply straightforward plan changes and bolt-ons.

Amber:

- Recommend a plan change based on usage patterns that is not obviously like-for-like.

- Draft offers to retain a customer at risk of churn, within a retention playbook.

Red:

- Decide complaint outcomes involving mis-selling or regulatory breaches.
- Handle complex disputes over contracts, credit reporting or disconnection.

The point is not to memorise these examples. It is to recognise that the same **Green / Amber / Red logic** holds up across sectors.

3.5 Work that should remain human-led

Some work should stay human-led for the foreseeable future, even if AI is involved in preparation.

Examples:

Life-changing decisions

- Accepting or denying access to essential services.
- Decisions that materially affect housing, healthcare, immigration or credit standing.

High-stakes vulnerability

- Cases involving domestic abuse, safeguarding, serious mental health issues or end-of-life care.
- Situations where language and nuance matter more than speed.

Serious complaints and remediation

- Final responses in regulated complaint processes.
- Decisions involving systemic failings, large remediation or public scrutiny.

Complex fraud and financial crime

- Investigations where patterns are ambiguous and stakes are high.
- Decisions that could unjustly deny someone access to financial services.

AI will still have a role here:

- Preparing case files.
- Summarising history.
- Highlighting patterns.
- Suggesting options within policy.

But the decision and accountability belong with humans. That is not simply a comfort choice; it is a governance choice.

3.6 Designing boundaries in practice

It is easy to draw a neat RAG diagram. Making it real requires you to:

1. **Start from journeys, not channels** Map a small set of journeys end-to-end. For each step, decide: Green, Amber or Red.
2. **Write the rule in one sentence** For each step, write a rule an advisor could repeat back. For example:

- "The assistant can set up any payment plan where the total term is under twelve months, and the monthly amount is at least £X."

- "The assistant can never close a complaint; it can only draft a summary and propose an outcome."

3. **Embed in tools and prompts** The RAG classification must not live only in a slide deck. It has to show up in:

   - Which tools the 'Agent' is allowed to call.
   - How prompts describe its role and limits.
   - How the UI (user interface) signals whether the assistant is executing, proposing or handing off.

4. **Test for edge cases** Use real transcripts and scenarios. Ask:

   - "What does the assistant do when the customer asks for more than policy allows?"
   - "What happens when someone refuses to go through security?"
   - "What if there are contradictory signals about vulnerability?"

If your tests only cover happy paths, your boundaries are theoretical.

3.7 Reviewing and moving boundaries

Boundaries are not static. As you gain evidence, some Amber work may move to Green; some over-ambitious Green work may need to move back to Amber or Red.

You should:

Review by intent, not by technology Examine metrics, errors, escalations and complaints for each intent, not for "the bot" overall.

Use clear criteria for promotion For example, to move from Amber to Green, you might require:

- Stable containment above an agreed threshold.
- No material increase in complaint rate.
- No new categories of error in your taxonomy.
- Sign-off from operations, risk and legal.

Be willing to reverse If complaint patterns change, risk appetite shifts or regulation tightens, move some work back from Green to Amber or Red. The architecture should make this reversible in days.

Boundaries are part of your risk posture. Treat them as such: explicit, reviewed, documented and adjustable.

3.8 How this connects to the rest of the book

This chapter has done three things:

- Shown that **patterns repeat across sectors** more than most organisations like to admit.
- Given you a simple **Red / Amber / Green boundary model** for AI roles.
- Highlighted the kind of work that should remain human-led, even when AI is present.

In the next chapter, we move from patterns to **customer journeys**, showing how to apply these boundaries step by step, so that AI, humans and systems each take on the work they are best suited to.

You should now be able to look at any proposed AI use case and ask, with more precision than "too risky" or "why not?":

- What pattern is this?
- Which steps are Green, Amber or Red?

- What would need to change – in policy, tools or knowledge – to move a step safely towards Green?

Those are the questions that separate AI experiments from AI operations.

Takeaway. The surface details of sectors differ; the work does not. Map demand to the seven families, wire the write-paths, keep bright boundaries, treat microcopy as a product, escalate cleanly, and measure only what guides decisions. Do this, and the assistant will resolve more, advisors will handle the right things, and your operation will feel calmer.

Chapter 4

The customer journey reimagined for AI and AI voice agents

This Chapter takes a single, familiar journey - a missed payment - and redesigns it from first principles for humans, AI and AI voice agents working together

Framework components:

- *Start with outcomes, not channels: target specific resolution outcomes and fewer failure loops.*
- *Canonical 'missed payment' journey:*
    - *Today: fragmented and reactive.*
    - *Desired: deliberate and joined up.*
- *Journey mapping discipline: triggers, states, decisions, data, owners.*
- *Assigning roles:*
    - *Design AI steps.*
    - *Design human steps.*
    - *Design system steps.*
- *Measuring the redesigned journey: containment, first contact resolution (FCR), escalations, complaints, time to resolution.*

- *Reusing the pattern: lift-and-shift method for other journeys.*
- *From slides to implementation: convert maps into backlog and change plan.*

4.1 Start with outcomes, not channels

Most transformation slides start with channels. Customers do not.

Customers start with a goal:

- "I need to update my address."
- "I can't afford this bill."
- "My order hasn't arrived."
- "I want to cancel this service."

Channels are just ways of saying these things.

If you design AI around channels, you end up with a chatbot project, a separate voice project, a separate email automation project and a separate 'social care' project, all solving the same underlying problems differently.

If you design around journeys, you can:

- Reuse patterns and tools across channels.
- Measure outcomes consistently.
- Decide, step by step, whether AI, humans or systems should take the lead.

This chapter is about that: taking one journey, making it brutally clear, and then showing how to redesign it so each part of the system does what it is best at.

We will use a single example throughout: **a missed payment journey in a regulated service**. The same logic applies to many other journeys.

4.2 A canonical journey: missed payment

Consider a customer who has missed a scheduled payment.

Their underlying goals are usually simple:

- Understand what has gone wrong.
- Avoid loss of service or more severe consequences.
- Find a way forward that they can actually keep to.

The organisation's goals are similarly simple:

- Collect what is owed where appropriate.
- Protect vulnerable customers.
- Stay within regulation and policy.
- Avoid unnecessary complaints and write-offs.

The trouble starts when nobody designs the journey end-to-end.

4.2.1 Today's journey: fragmented and reactive

A typical 'as-is' missed payment journey looks like this:

5. System flags a missed payment and generates standard outbound messages.

6. Some customers ignore them because the language is confusing or they are overwhelmed.

7. Some call in; others use chat, email or social media to say "I'm struggling" in one of a hundred different ways.

8. Advisors improvise within policy, with varying comfort and skill.

9. Some customers are put on plans they cannot afford; some are not told all their options.

10. Systems record fragments of the story in different places.

11. Collections and complaints teams deal with the consequences later.

Common symptoms:

- High repeat contact.
- Inconsistent outcomes for similar customers.
- Difficult QA (quality assurance) and compliance reviews.
- Advisors avoiding these calls because they are emotionally heavy and the advisors are poorly supported.

4.2.2 Desired journey: deliberate and joined-up

A deliberately designed journey starts with:

- Clear entry conditions (what counts as 'missed payment').
- Clear segmentation (e.g. first-time vs repeated, amount vs income, existing flags).

- Clear options and red lines.
- Clear roles for AI, humans and systems.

A simple high-level target state might be:

1. Detect missed payment and trigger a structured outbound journey.
2. Use AI to have the first conversation: explain, listen, structure options.
3. Keep humans in the loop where affordability, vulnerability or edge cases appear.
4. Record a complete, structured history so later teams see context, not just balances.
5. Track outcomes over time: cure rates, re-defaults, complaints, write-offs.

The job of AI here is not to squeeze customers harder. It is to make the early interaction clearer, more consistent and less dependent on who happens to pick up the phone.

4.3 Mapping the journey step by step

To redesign any journey, you need one simple artefact: a step-by-step map that everyone agrees on.

A minimal template:

Step	Customer intent	System state / trigger	Current behaviour (typical)	Problems
1	Customer misses payment	Payment fails/due date passes	Auto-message sent with generic wording	Confusing tone, poor engagement
2	Customer receives message	Message delivered	Some ignore, some call, some go online	Many channels, no consistent handling
3	Customer contacts organisation	Inbound contact created	Routed via IVR / menus to general queue	Repetition, long explanations, variable outcomes
4	Advisor or bot explores situation	Account and history in multiple systems	Free-text questions, varied depth	Inconsistent affordability and vulnerability checks
5	Plan or outcome agreed	Agreement recorded in partial form	Notes in CRM; sometimes separate spreadsheet	Hard to audit, hard to track performance
6	Follow-up and monitoring	Payment plan live	Ad-hoc follow-up; some automated reminders	Weak early warning for re-defaults

The point of this table is not aesthetics. It is to make visible where:

- Information is missing.
- Work is duplicated.
- Decisions vary without good reason.
- Customers fall between cracks.

You cannot sensibly add AI to a journey you have not mapped.

4.4 Assigning roles: AI, humans, systems

Once the steps are clear, you can assign roles using the Red / Amber / Green logic from the previous chapter.

For the missed payment journey, a simplified assignment might be:

Step	Description	Zone	AI role	Human role	System role
1	Detect missed payment	Green	None (event-driven)	None	Detect event; raise flag
2	Inform and invite conversation	Green	Generate tailored, plain-language messages	Set templates and policy	Deliver via channel; log contact
3	First inbound/outbound contact	Green	Explain situation; gather facts; check identity	Intervene only on escalation	Provide data to AI
4	Explore affordability & context	Amber	Structure discussion; capture income/expense; propose options	Review proposals on flagged cases	Store data; run affordability rules
5	Agree plan or next step	Amber	Apply standard options and summarise in plain English	Approve or adjust at edge of policy or high risk	Record plan; set up schedule
6	Follow up and monitor	Green	Remind, check-in, capture early distress signals	Handle escalations or significant changes	Track payments; trigger alerts
7	Handle breakdown or complaint	Red	Summarise history; draft options	Decide outcomes, especially on complaints and vulnerability	Provide full timeline and data

A few points:

- Steps 2, 3 and 6 are strong candidates for AI-first, with human support.
- Step 4 and 5 sit in Amber; AI can structure and propose, but humans approve when risk is higher.
- Step 7 stays Red: humans own complaint and serious risk decisions.

This is how you stop 'AI' becoming an abstract conversation. You determine which steps move to AI-first; which become AI-assisted human; and which remain human-only.

4.5 Designing the AI part of the journey

For each step where AI plays a role, you need three things:

1. **A clear goal, from the customer's perspective**

- "I understand why I owe this, what my options are and what happens next."

2. **A micro-plan for the agentic loop**

- Listen → Plan → Retrieve → Act → Check → Summarise → Decide.

3. **A small set of tools and guardrails**

- Tools to fetch balances, history, flags, and to create payment links or plans.
- Guardrails on what the assistant may and may not offer.

For example, at the ‘explore affordability & context’ step:

- The assistant should ask structured but human-sounding questions.
- It should map answers into a standard format (income, fixed commitments, variable spends, recent shocks).
- It should run those through a policy-based calculator to determine what options are in-bounds.
- If the situation looks complex or high-risk (e.g. clear signs of acute vulnerability), it should escalate with a complete summary.

Success here is not ‘the AI sounded good’. It is:

- Customers feel heard and informed.
- Advisors report that escalations arrive with complete, useful context.
- Plans agreed via this path have lower re-default rates than the old process.

4.6 Designing the human part of the journey

When AI takes on more of the repetitive and structured work, human roles need to change consciously, not accidentally.

In the missed payment journey, advisors should:

- Spend less time re-collecting basic facts.
- Spend more time on tricky affordability, vulnerability and negotiation.

- Become decision-makers and advocates inside policy, not just script-followers.

To support that, you need:

- **Clear playbooks** for higher-risk scenarios, written with the same discipline you used for AI guardrails.
- **Simple on-screen summaries** that show the assistant's work: what was said, what was offered, what was chosen or declined.
- **Authority and limits** that are clear: when an advisor can override, and when they must refer up.

A good handoff packet for a missed payment case might include:

- Identity status and method.
- Customer's stated goal, in their own words.
- Income and expense summary.
- Available options and which were offered.
- Signals of vulnerability or distress.
- The assistant's recommended next step, clearly labelled as a suggestion.

Human work gets harder, not easier, when AI is added without these supports. The point of redesign is to make human work both more effective and more sustainable.

4.7 Designing the system's part of the journey

Systems have three jobs that humans and AI cannot do alone:

1. **Be the source of truth**

- One place to check balances, flags, plans and outcomes.
- Versioned, auditable records of what happened, when and why.

2. **Run scheduled work reliably**

- Payment schedules.
- Reminder cycles.
- Reports and alerts.

3. **Provide facts to both AI and humans**

- Consistent APIs that do not change without notice.
- Fields that are well-defined and reliably populated.

In many organisations, the blocker to a better journey is not 'AI capability' but:

- No clean way to set up a payment plan via API.
- No consistent place to record vulnerability flags.
- No shared identifier that ties channels together.

Journey redesign is often the moment where these gaps become impossible to ignore.

4.8 Measuring the redesigned journey

A redesigned journey is only an improvement if the numbers move.

For a missed payment journey, useful measures include:

1. **Containment by intent**
   - Percentage of customers who complete the journey without needing a further contact in a set period.
2. **Time to reassurance**
   - How long before a customer hears a clear statement like: "You will not be disconnected while you keep to this plan."
3. **Payment outcomes**
   - Cure rates (customers who bring accounts back into order).
   - Re-default rates (how many plans break, and how quickly).
4. **Human work profile**
   - Minutes per escalated case.
   - Quality and completeness of case notes.
5. **Experience and risk**
   - CSAT for these journeys.
   - Complaint rates linked to missed payments.
   - Incidents related to affordability or vulnerability handling.

For economics, you can express CPR for the journey as:

CPR = (AI handling minutes × AI cost per minute) + (human handling minutes × human cost per minute) divided by number of fully resolved cases.

A simple sensitivity check:

- If AI containment improves by ±10% from your forecast, what happens to CPR and complaint rates?
- If escalated case AHT is ±10% different from your assumption, does the business case still hold?

This is how you keep the journey honest.

4.9 Reusing the pattern

The same design approach works for other journeys:

Change of address

- Clean Green steps (verify identity, update address, confirm downstream effects).
- Clear Red zones (changes affecting ownership, security, or regulated documents).

Broken product in retail

- Green: capture issue, confirm purchase, initiate standard replacements and refunds.
- Amber: goodwill beyond standard, discretionary gifts.
- Red: systemic safety issues, fraud patterns.

Technical fault in telecoms

- Green: guided diagnostic steps, simple resets, status checks.
- Amber: booking engineer visits, managing expectations on SLAs.

- Red: cases involving safety, vulnerable customers or repeated failure.

Once you have one journey properly redesigned, you can:

- Reuse guardrail patterns.
- Reuse data and tool patterns.
- Reuse measurement templates.

The work gets easier with each additional journey, provided you resist the urge to create a completely new approach each time.

4.10 From slides to implementation

A redesigned journey on a wall is the easy part.

To make it real, you need:

A small, cross-functional squad

- Operations, risk/compliance, technology, data, frontline representation.
- One accountable owner.

A clear scope for the first slice

- One journey, a defined segment, a limited channel set if needed.

A build and test plan

- Tools and write-paths created or improved.
- Guardrails and prompts written, tested and approved.

- Dark launches, canary traffic, clear rollback.

A review cycle

- Weekly or fortnightly reviews of metrics, error types and case studies.
- Iterations that retire one failure mode at a time.

If you cannot name the owner, the squad, the scope and the review rhythm, you do not have a redesign; you have an aspiration.

This chapter has shown how to move from abstract talk of 'customer experience' to concrete, redesigned journeys where AI, humans and systems each have defined roles. In the next chapter, we focus on the human side of that arrangement: how AI changes frontline work, skills, training and trust, and what leaders must do to keep people engaged rather than threatened.

Takeaway. Reimagining the customer journey is not about adding channels or clever widgets. It is about **shortening the path from intent to outcome** with clarity, control and respect. Verify once. Plan small. Act and prove. Stop gracefully when you should. Escalate with continuity. Measure only what you will use. Do this, and customers will describe your service as easy, advisors will finish faster, and the numbers will justify the investment.

Chapter 5

Human, AI and AI voice agents working together

The purpose of this Chapter is to define the operating model for blended teams.

Main framework: three operating models:

- *AI-assisted human: agent in control, AI as copilot.*
- *Human-assisted AI: AI in front, humans handle edge cases.*
- *AI-first with human fallback: maximum concurrency with a safety net.*

Supporting elements:

- *Not 'versus' but 'who does what': division of labour, not a fight.*
- *What agents need in order to trust the system: transparency, predictable behaviour, clear escalation, feedback loops.*
- *The first 30 days for frontline: training, pilots, support.*
- *New roles and skills: AI supervisors, knowledge owners, playbook/prompt owners.*

- *Supervision and feedback loops: how humans oversee and improve AI output.*
- *Performance management: metrics that reflect AI and human contributions.*
- *Culture, communication, resistance: avoid 'the robots are coming for you' narratives.*
- *What changes for leadership: new questions and oversight linked to ethics and guardrails.*

5.1 Not 'versus', but 'who does what?'

The least useful question in this space is: "Will AI replace agents?"

It sounds dramatic and keeps event panels busy, but it does not help you design an operation. The real question is:

- **What work should people do?**
- **What work should AI do?**
- **What work should systems do?**

The answer will differ by journey, but three principles hold:

1. People are better at context, judgement, emotion and escalation.
2. AI is better at pattern recognition, retrieval, summarisation and structured decisioning within rules.
3. Systems are better at being the source of truth and executing repeatable actions.

If you do not make these distinctions explicit, AI projects will quietly push more complexity and emotional load onto humans while claiming cost savings in presentations. This chapter is about avoiding that.

5.2 Three operating models

There are three basic ways to combine humans and AI in service operations.

You should be able to point at any journey and say which of these you are using.

5.2.1 AI-assisted human

Primary owner: Human
AI role: Co-pilot and assistant

The advisor (human) is in control of the interaction.

The AI:

- Listens and suggests next best actions.
- Surfaces relevant knowledge and past interactions.
- Drafts notes, emails or summaries.
- Checks compliance steps and flags gaps.

This model works well when:

- The work is complex or nuanced.
- The customer expects continuity with a named advisor.
- The organisation is early in its AI maturity and wants low-regret gains.

Risks if badly implemented:

- Screen clutter and cognitive overload.

- Advisors ignoring suggestions because they are poor quality.

- No clear ownership when AI advice is followed and goes wrong.

Done well, this model is a low-drama way to improve quality and consistency without changing the front door.

5.2.2 Human-assisted AI

Primary owner: AI
Human role: Supervisor and exception handler

The assistant (AI) handles the majority of contacts within clearly defined journeys.

Humans:

- Take over when the work moves outside guardrails.

- Review and approve decisions in Amber zones.

- Handle complaints, risk and high-stakes vulnerability.

This model works well when:

- Intents are well-understood and relatively structured.

- You have good tools and knowledge, not just a clever model.

- You have clear escalation and handoff patterns.

Risks if badly implemented:

- Customers feel trapped behind an unhelpful bot.

- Escalations arrive with poor context, forcing repetition.

- Advisors feel reduced to "clean-up crew" for failed automation.

Done well, this model carries a substantial chunk of demand while maintaining quality and control.

5.2.3 AI-first with human fallback

Primary owner:
AI for Green steps; shared for Amber; human for Red

Human role:
Decision-maker where stakes or ambiguity are high

This is the mixed model that tends to emerge as you scale. It looks like:

- AI resolving simple journeys end-to-end.
- AI and humans collaborating on Amber work (AI proposes; human approves).
- Humans owning Red decisions, with strong prep and summaries from AI.

This model works when:

- You have a clear RAG (Red/Amber/Green) classification by step.
- You can show, with evidence, that Green steps are safe.
- You have the discipline to move steps back if the data tells you to.

Risks if badly implemented:

- Everything being declared Green for convenience.

- Nobody remembering why something was classified the way it was.
- Change control becoming chaotic.

The rest of this chapter assumes you are heading towards this mixed model. If you pretend otherwise, reality will correct you.

5.3 What agents need in order to trust the system

Frontline teams decide, quietly, whether your AI projects succeed.

They know where the bodies are buried in your processes. They see what actually happens when customers are confused, upset or angry. If they do not trust the tools, they will:

- Work around them.
- Switch them off when nobody is watching.
- Give negative informal feedback that kills adoption.

Agents need five things to trust AI:

1. **Transparency**

- They can see what the AI Assistant did, what it assumed and what it used as a source.
- They can understand, at least at a high level, why a recommendation was made.

2. **Control**

- They can override or correct the 'Assistant' when it is wrong, without wrestling the system.

- Overrides are logged, not punished.

3. **Responsiveness**

- Feedback changes something. If advisors regularly correct a particular pattern, they see it improve.

4. **Protection**

- They are not held personally responsible for good-faith use of tools that were signed off by leadership.
- Performance metrics do not punish them for work mix shifting towards harder cases.

5. **Clarity**

- They know, in plain English, what the 'Assistant' is allowed to do and where they must step in.

You cannot buy this trust with a training deck. You earn it by how you design, deploy and respond.

5.4 The first 30 days for frontline

The first month of a deployment is where most trust is won or lost.

A pragmatic plan:

Week 1: Orientation and honest framing

- Explain the journey(s) being changed, not 'AI in general'.
- Show the RAG map and what the assistant will and will not do.

Be explicit:

- “You will see fewer of [these contacts].”
- “You will see more of [these types of escalations].”
- Confirm that good-faith use of the new system will not be used as ammunition in performance reviews.

Week 2: Shadow mode

Let advisors see the ’Assistant’s’ proposed responses, actions and summaries in real time, without sending them to customers.

Ask them to mark:

- “Would send as-is.”
- “Would send with changes.”
- “Would not send; unsafe or wrong.”
- Use this to refine prompts, knowledge and tools before full go-live.

Week 3: Assisted live

Allow the ’Assistant’ to send messages or take actions, with advisors supervising and correcting.

Capture examples where:

- AI clearly added value.
- AI made understandable but wrong calls.
- AI made worrying errors (data, tone, compliance).

Week 4: Normalised operations

Move into standard operating mode, with:

- Clear escalation routes.
- Transparent metrics shared with advisors.
- Standing forums (e.g. weekly surgeries) where frontline feedback is heard and acted upon.

The message should be: "We are changing how work works, and we are doing it with you, not to you."

5.5 New roles and skills

As you scale AI in service, you will see new roles emerge. You can either pretend they do not exist and let people muddle through or make them explicit.

Common roles:

Journey owner

- Accountable for performance of a specific journey end-to-end, not just their department's slice.
- Looks at intent volumes, containment, CPR, CSAT, complaints and error patterns.
- Agrees changes with risk and technology.

AI champion/super-user

- Experienced advisor who understands both the work and the tools.
- Collects frontline feedback, helps resolve issues and contributes to tuning.

- Often the most credible voice in training sessions.

Quality & safety reviewer

- Samples AI-handled and AI-assisted interactions.
- Classifies errors using a simple taxonomy.
- Works with journey owners to eliminate recurring issues.

Prompt & knowledge maintainer

Not a mystical 'prompt engineer', but someone who:

- Updates guardrails and prompts under change control.
- Keeps knowledge fresh and aligned with policy.
- Works closely with risk, legal and operations.

Skills that rise in importance for frontline staff:

- Comfort working alongside a system that suggests and automates.
- Ability to handle a higher mix of complex and emotionally loaded cases.
- Familiarity with basic data and metrics (intent, containment, AHT, CPR).
- Confidence in escalating when something feels wrong, even if the system says it is fine.

Good people adapt. But they adapt faster and with less attrition when you recognise and support these shifts.

5.6 Supervision and feedback loops

'Human in the loop' is not a slogan; it is a design choice.

You need to know:

- Where humans can intervene.
- What tools they have to do so.
- How their interventions flow back into system improvement.

A simple feedback loop:

Event

An AI-handled or AI-assisted interaction occurs.

Sampling

You sample interactions based on:

- Risk (e.g. complaints, high-value cases).
- Random selection.
- Signals (e.g. low CSAT, long handle times).

Classification

Reviewers classify issues using a small taxonomy:

- Misunderstood intent.
- Wrong or incomplete knowledge.
- Tool misuse or failure.

- Poor tone or lack of empathy.
- Guardrail breach.
- Escalation too late or too early.

Action

Each class has default owners:

- Operations for process changes.
- Knowledge owners for content changes.
- Technology for tools and prompts.
- Risk for boundary and policy issues.

Verification

- You check, after changes, whether the same class of error has reduced.

Without this structure, feedback from agents and customers simply leaks away. You get frustration, not improvement.

5.7 Performance management in a blended world

If you change the work but not the metrics, you punish the people you expect to carry the change.

Common traps:

- **Holding advisors to old AHT targets** when their case mix has shifted towards harder work.
- **Rewarding only volume** when quality and risk management have become more important.

- **Ignoring contribution to system improvement** (e.g. good feedback, error spotting).

Better patterns:

Separate metrics by work type

- Distinguish between escalated AI cases, legacy cases and pure human journeys in your MI (management information).
- Compare like with like.

Include quality and safety

Build:

- Error-rate views by journey.
- Complaints and remediation data.
- Compliance outcomes.

Recognise triage and escalation judgement

- Identifying and escalating risk appropriately is a skill, not an error. Treat it as such.

For AI itself, you should:

- Avoid vanity metrics (eg: '99% accuracy') with no clear definition.
- Focus on impact measures: containment, CPR, CSAT, complaint rates, error distributions.

Performance management should reinforce the behaviours you actually want: collaboration with the system, honest feedback, and care with higher-stakes work.

5.8 Culture, communication and resistance

Resistance to AI is often described as fear of replacement. Sometimes it is just rational scepticism.

Frontline staff have seen:

- Tools launched, then abandoned.
- Process changes that made their lives harder.
- Metrics used selectively to justify decisions already made.

If you want a different reaction this time, you will need to behave differently.

Practical commitments you can make:

No surprises

- Communicate early, with specifics.
- Share the journeys being targeted, the expected impacts and the uncertainties.

No punishment for honest use

- Make it clear that if an advisor uses the tools as trained, leadership owns the risk.

Visible response to feedback

- Show, with concrete examples, where frontline feedback led to changes.
- Close the loop: "You told us X; here is what we did; here is what changed."

Leaders using their own tools

- Senior leaders should see real interactions, not just dashboards and summaries.

When possible, let them use internal versions of the tools.

An honest message is more effective than sugar-coating. It is reasonable to say:

"Some of the work we do today will move to AI. The work left for people will often be more complex, more skilled and more emotionally demanding. Our job as leaders is to equip and support you for that reality, not pretend it is not happening."

5.9 What changes for leadership

Leaders do not get to stay in the old pattern either.

Key shifts:

- From "How big is the team?" to "What mix of AI, humans and systems do we need for each journey?"
- From 'call centre management' to 'journey ownership across channels and tools'.

From occasional fire drills to continuous, controlled change.

Practically, leaders need to:

- Learn enough about AI and architecture to ask sensible questions.
- Read Management Information that includes AI performance, not just human performance.
- Sponsor cross-functional squads that own journeys, not just departmental KPIs.
- Set and review risk appetite in a way that matches the RAG model in Chapter 3.

You cannot delegate understanding of AI entirely to technology or data teams. The decisions are operational and commercial as much as technical.

5.10 Connecting to ethics, law and guardrails

This chapter has focused on people and operating models. It assumes that someone has written and enforced a clear rulebook for AI.

The next chapter makes that explicit.

We will move from “Who does what?” to “What the system is and is not allowed to do”, covering:

- Transparency and disclosure.
- Lawful basis, consent and data minimisation.
- Vulnerable customers and red lines.
- Auditability, logging and evidence.
- Kill switches and rollback plans.

Human and AI collaboration only works if both are operating inside rules that are understandable and enforceable. Otherwise, you are just distributing risk more quickly.

Takeaway. Blending works when lanes are clear, handoffs are respectful, knowledge behaves like software and numbers are small and honest. The assistant starts early and stops early when it should. People finish without friction. Peaks are quieter, decisions are cleaner, and the culture gets calmer.

Chapter 6

Ethics, law and the guardrails that make AI safe to scale

In this Chapter we show how to turn ethics and law into a usable guardrail stack.

Key frameworks:

- *Why this is not optional: risk, regulators, reputation and licence to operate.*
- *Legal frame in plain language: lawful basis, purpose limitation, necessity, proportionality.*
- *The guardrail stack: policy, design controls, runtime controls, monitoring, incident response.*
- *Purpose, scope, disclosure: clarity on what AI does, where, and how users are informed.*
- *Identity, access, vulnerability: rules for who you are dealing with and how you protect them.*
- *Data, privacy, retention: logging, retention windows, redaction, minimisation.*
- *Language, behaviour, vulnerability: tone guidelines, behavioural guardrails, escalation triggers.*
- *Payments and money movement: no card capture, secure links, keep AI out of PCI scope.*

- *Logging, monitoring, audit: what to capture and review.*
- *Kill switch, rollback, incidents: operational reverse gear.*

Working with risk, legal, compliance: co-design instead of block-and-fight; tie ethics to commercial outcomes.

6.1 Why this is not a side-quest

Most AI project builders spend too long on the model and too little on the rulebook.

Ethics and law are often treated as a separate workstream: something you 'run past legal' once the interesting part is done. That is backwards. In customer service, ethics and law are the work:

- You are talking to real people about real money, services and rights.
- You are handling personal data, often sensitive.
- You are operating under regulators who have long memories and sharp teeth.

Handled well, ethics and law become a design advantage:

- Clear guardrails make it easier to move faster without constant escalation.
- Well-structured evidence makes it easier to defend decisions.
- Customers and staff trust systems that behave consistently and visibly within rules.

Handled badly, you get:

- Quiet bans on AI from your own risk and legal teams who no longer trust you.
- Expensive remediation projects.
- Public embarrassment and regulatory intervention.

This chapter sets out a guardrail stack you can explain to boards, regulators and staff without needing a law degree.

6.2 The legal frame in plain language

The specifics vary by sector, but in the UK most customer operations sit inside three layers:

Data protection and privacy

- UK GDPR and the Data Protection Act 2018.
- Core ideas: lawful basis, purpose limitation, data minimisation, accuracy, storage limitation, integrity, confidentiality and accountability.

Sector regulation and conduct

- Requirements from bodies such as the FCA, Ofcom, Ofgem, the ICO and health, transport or other industry regulators.
- Themes: fair treatment, clear communication, suitability, vulnerability, affordability, dispute handling and record-keeping.

General law and contract

- Contracts, consumer protection, unfair terms, negligence, discrimination and misuse of confidential information.

This book does not try to restate the law. Its position is simpler:

- Design your AI so that, if a regulator or court asks, "Why did this happen?", you can answer with **evidence, not vibes**.
- Assume that every decision you make in the build may one day need to be explained to a sceptical audience.

To do that, you need guardrails.

6.3 The guardrail stack

A useful way to think about guardrails is as a stack:

1. **Purpose & scope**

   - What this assistant is for, and what it is not for.

2. **Disclosure & consent**

   - What you tell people about the assistant and their data.

3. **Identity & access**

   - How you decide who you are dealing with and what they can see or do.

4. **Data & retention**

   - What you collect, store, share and delete.

5. **Language & behaviour**

   - How the assistant talks, what it will not say and how it treats vulnerable customers.

6. **Tools & write-paths**

   - What systems it can actually change and under what conditions.

7. **Logging, monitoring & audit**

   - What you record, how you sample and what you review.

8. **Kill switch & rollback**

   - How you stop, unwind and learn from problems.

Each layer should exist in three forms:

- A short, plain-English policy.
- Concrete examples or scenarios.
- Technical implementation (prompts, configuration, code, dashboards).

If a layer exists in a presentation slide deck or only in a prompt, it does not exist.

6.4 Purpose, scope and disclosure

Start by being boringly specific.

For each assistant, write a one-page **purpose and scope note**:

Primary purpose

- e.g. 'To help existing customers understand and manage their account, including balances, payments and simple changes.'

Out of scope

- e.g. 'No advice on regulated investments; no decisions on service disconnection; no changes to beneficial ownership; no diagnostic clinical advice.'

Supported journeys

- List the specific intents and journeys, with links to owners.

RAG classification

- Map each step in each journey as Green, Amber or Red (from Chapter 3).

Then define disclosure rules:

Always tell people they are dealing with an AI assistant.

- Early in the interaction, in plain language.

Without theatrical names that imply human judgement where there is none.

Always offer a path to a human.

- Be honest about availability and expected wait times.

- Do not hide escalation behind trick questions.

Explain data use at an appropriate level.

- You do not have to recite privacy notices in full, but you must not mislead.
- A short, accurate statement about what is being used - and for what - is usually enough, with a link to more.
- If you are embarrassed to say plainly what the assistant is and does, you have designed it wrong.

6.5 Identity, access and vulnerability

Identity and access are where many breaches and complaints begin.

Guardrails here should cover:

Verification levels

Define levels such as:

- Unverified: can only receive general information.
- Partially verified: can discuss some account-level information.
- Fully verified: can make and approve changes.

State what is required for each level (e.g. known facts, OTP, document checks by humans).

Channel-specific rules

- Decide what can and cannot be disclosed or changed via each channel.

- For example, you might ban certain disclosures over open messaging channels, regardless of verification.

Acting for someone else

- Rules for authorised representatives, powers of attorney, carers and family members.
- The 'Assistant' should know when to stop and hand off.

Vulnerability signals and flags

- How the 'Assistant' detects potential vulnerability (words, behaviour, history).
- What it must do when it detects them: slow down, explain more, escalate, or all three.
- How vulnerability is recorded, reviewed and used to adapt future interactions.

Principle:

If you would not allow a new human agent to make a change after the level of questioning and checking used, do not allow the AI to make it either.

Test this. Take transcripts and ask your risk and frontline teams:

- "Would this level of checking be acceptable from a human?"
- "Would we stand by this in front of a regulator or ombudsman?"

If the answer is no, change the rules.

6.6 Data, privacy and retention

You cannot be 'good at AI' and sloppy with data.

Guardrails should specify:

Data minimisation

- What data the 'Assistant' is allowed to collect.
- What data it is allowed to view.
- What data it is never allowed to ask for or store (e.g. full card numbers, security answers in free text).

Purpose limitation

- Clear descriptions of why data is used.
- No quiet repurposing into other uses without governance (e.g. training unrelated models).

Storage and retention

- How long interaction data, transcripts and derived features are kept.
- Different retention for operational use vs training or analysis, if needed.
- Process for deletion or anonymisation.

Access control

- Which roles can see what.
- Use of least privilege, including for admin tools.

Third parties

- What leaves your environment and under what agreements.
- How you ensure they meet your standards.

In practice, this means you should be able to answer questions such as:

- "Show me all the data this assistant has about me and why it is held."
- "Delete or restrict my data where I have the right to request it."
- "Explain why this data was used to make this decision."

If you cannot, you have a data governance problem, not an AI problem.

6.7 Language, behaviour and vulnerable customers

'Assistants' represent your organisation, not themselves.

Guardrails for language and behaviour should include:

Tone & style

- Neutral, clear, respectful.
- No faux empathy that trivialises serious situations.
- No bluffing: if the 'Assistant' does not know, it should say so and escalate.

Prohibited behaviour

- No threats beyond what policy and regulation explicitly allow.
- No discrimination based on protected characteristics.
- No pressure tactics on vulnerable customers.

Vulnerability behaviour

Specific instructions on what to do when someone:

- Mentions suicidal thoughts or self-harm.
- Mentions abuse, coercion or threats.
- Appears confused, distressed or unable to process information.

Provide clear escalation paths and scripts for these cases.

Error honesty

If something has gone wrong (e.g. duplicate charges, missed appointments), the 'Assistant' should:

- Acknowledge it.
- Avoid defensive language.
- Move quickly to resolution or escalation.

Underlying idea:

It is better to be obviously limited and honest than fluent and misleading.

You can test this by having humans role-play difficult scenarios and comparing the assistant's performance to what you would accept from a trained advisor.

6.8 Payments and money movement

Payments are high-risk and emotionally loaded.

Guardrails should enforce that:

'Assistants' never directly handle card details.

- They use secure payment links or redirect to approved payment flows.
- They do not ask customers to type full card numbers into open chat.

All payment options are within approved policy.

- No invented plans or unapproved discounts.
- Clear limits and thresholds for automated offers.

Affordability and vulnerability checks are not optional.

- Where you have obligations to assess affordability or support vulnerable customers, the assistant must follow those steps consistently.

Receipts and confirmations are clear.

- Customers should receive a record of what they agreed, what will happen and how to get help if they cannot keep to a plan.

Disputes and chargebacks are handled with care.

- The 'Assistant' may collect details and explain process, but final decisions in complex cases should remain human.

Money-handling flows should be among the most heavily tested and monitored journeys you have.

6.9 Logging, monitoring and audit

If you cannot reconstruct what happened, you are not in control.

At a minimum, you should log:

Who

- An identifier for the customer or user.
- The assistant identity (version, environment).

What

- Full interaction text or transcript.
- Tools used, with inputs and outputs.
- Knowledge objects consulted (and their versions).
- Decisions taken, including whether or not to escalate.

When

- Timestamps for key events: start, tool calls, escalations, end.

Why (as far as possible)

- Reason codes for outcomes.
- Error codes for failures.
- Flags for vulnerability, complaint or risk.

Monitoring should provide:

Operational MI

- Intent volumes, containment, AHT, latency, CPR and VPR.
- Escalation rates and reasons.

Quality & safety MI

- Error distributions by type.
- Complaint rates and themes involving AI journeys.
- Vulnerability handling outcomes.

Change MI

- What changed (prompts, tools, knowledge).
- When it changed.
- What impact it had on the above metrics.

Audit should be able to:

- Pull samples by intent, date range, outcome or risk flag.
- Trace each interaction through to the data and rules applied.
- Understand who signed off changes and why.

If audit cannot get what it needs, it is only a matter of time before a regulator has the same problem.

6.10 Kill switch, rollback and incidents

Systems fail. AI is no exception.

Guardrails must include:

Kill switches

- The ability to stop specific journeys or 'Assistants' quickly without taking everything offline.
- Just-in-case scenarios defined in advance (e.g. certain error patterns, spikes in complaints, discovered policy breach).

Rollback plans

For each journey, a clear 'back to last safe state' plan:

- What you will turn off.
- What you will revert to (e.g. human-only handling).
- How you will communicate the change internally.

Incident categories and playbooks

For example:

- Data leakage.
- Systemic miscalculation (e.g. wrong charges or eligibility).
- Complaints spike.
- Reputational incident (e.g. a widely shared transcript).

Each with:

- Owners.
- Steps to investigate, contain and remediate.

Requirements to notify regulators or affected customers where applicable.

Post-incident reviews

- Blameless but candid analysis.
- Specific changes to tools, knowledge, guardrails or training.
- Clear record of what was learned.

If your incident process treats AI as "special" and separate from other operational incidents, you will miss links and repeat mistakes. Fold it into your existing risk and incident machinery.

6.11 Working with risk, legal and compliance

Risk, legal and compliance functions are not obstacles; they are the only reason you get to keep operating.

To keep them as partners rather than blockers:

Involve them early.

- Bring them into intent and journey selection, not just sign-off.
- Share prototypes and early metrics, not just polished decks.

Speak their language.

Come with:

- Purpose and scope notes.
- RAG classifications.
- Guardrail summaries.
- DPIA and related assessments where required.

Show how you will evidence control, not just that you 'understand the law'.

Agree review rhythms.

- Regular check-ins on metrics, incidents and boundary changes.
- Named individuals with authority to approve and halt.

Treat them as users of the system.

- Give them access to the MI they need.
- Let them pull samples and trace decisions without heroic effort.

The best sign that your governance is working is not the absence of issues. It is the presence of small issues that are caught early, classified, fixed and learned from.

6.12 Connecting ethics, law and commercial outcomes

Ethics and law are often framed as a cost or a brake. In reality:

- Clear guardrails mean fewer escalations, faster approvals and less wasted effort.
- Good evidence means less time lost in arguments and reconstruction exercises.
- Trusted systems mean customers are more willing to use self-service and automation.

The choice is not between fast AI and safe AI. It is between:

- AI that looks fast until something breaks and you have to stop suddenly.
- AI that is safe enough to keep running while you improve it.

This chapter has laid out the guardrail stack and the behaviours that make it real. The next chapter turns back to the money: building business cases that boards can actually sign off on, using the same disciplines and evidence that keep regulators on side.

Takeaway. Ethics and law are not obstacles to progress; they are how you move fast **without** breaking the people who trust you. Publish one rulebook. Keep data small and justified. Draw bright boundaries. Prefer decisions you can reverse. Measure what matters and retire one error class a week. Do that and you'll have a service that customers accept, regulators respect and leaders can scale without flinching.

Chapter 7

Building the business case that boards actually approve

*In this Chapter we p*rovide a board-ready business case template.

Framework:

- *What boards care about: risk, cost, revenue, customer outcomes.*
- *Business case skeleton: problem, baseline, intervention, benefits, costs, risk, decision gates.*
- *Getting the baseline right: volumes, CPR, average handling time (AHT), repeat contact, complaints, churn, bad debt.*
- *Describing the intervention: journeys, segments, models, guardrails.*
- *Costing the change: build, run, people, partners, platforms.*
- *Modelling the benefits: simple formulas, ranges, sensitivities.*
- *Linking pilots to the business case: using pilot metrics to test assumptions.*
- *Governance, RACI, decision gates: who decides, when, and on what evidence.*
- *Common AI business case failure modes: overclaim, under-baseline, ignoring risk and change costs.*

- *Framing AI in the boardroom: storyline that connects to optimisation and ongoing value.*

7.1 What boards actually care about

Boards and executive committees do not approve 'AI projects'.

They approve changes to how money, risk and reputation are managed. In customer service, that usually boils down to a small set of questions:

- What problem are we solving, in numbers not adjectives?
- What will change in how we serve customers and manage risk?
- What will it cost, today and over time?
- What will it save or earn, and how confident are we?
- How will we know it is working, and how do we stop if it is not?

If your AI business case does not answer these directly, you are asking for a leap of faith. Most boards have used up their tolerance for faith-based technology.

This chapter sets out a simple business case structure and the disciplines that make it credible.

7.2 The business case skeleton

Every AI business case in customer service should be able to fit on one page before it expands to the detail.

A practical skeleton:

Problem statement

The specific journeys and metrics that are underperforming.

Baseline

Current volumes, costs, outcomes and risk indicators.

Intervention

- The journeys to be redesigned, the operating model (AI vs human vs systems) and the guardrail posture.

Costs

- One-off and recurring costs for people, technology and change.

Benefits

- Expected changes in volume, mix, CPR (cost per resolution), VPR (value per resolution), risk and experience.

Sensitivities and scenarios

- What happens if key assumptions (e.g. containment, AHT, adoption) are ±10–20% from expectation.

Risks and mitigations

- Key operational, legal, regulatory and people risks, and how they will be controlled.

Implementation plan & governance

- 90-day plan, decision gates, owners and kill switches.

If you cannot fill this out clearly, you are not ready for approval. If you can, the rest of the document is just supporting detail.

7.3 Getting the baseline right

Baselines are where most business cases go soft.

You need a baseline at the level where AI will actually operate: by **intent and journey**, not just by channel.

For each targeted journey, capture:

Volumes

- Contacts per period by intent, across channels.
- Seasonality and peak patterns.

Outcomes

- Containment (how many are fully resolved in-channel).
- FCR (first-contact resolution).
- Transfers and escalations.

- Complaint rates and remediation.

Time and cost

- Average handle time (AHT), including talk, wrap and follow-up.
- Total handling minutes per resolved case.

CPR

- CPR = (total handling minutes × cost per minute) / number of resolved cases

Value

- VPR where applicable (e.g. revenue retained, debt collected, bad debt avoided, churn avoided).
- The negative side: cost of failure (e.g. write-offs, compensation, regulatory fines, reputational damage where you can sensibly approximate).

This is rarely all available in a neat dashboard. You may need:

- Sampled time-and-motion studies.
- Data from multiple systems stitched together.
- Assumptions agreed with finance and operations.

The key is to write assumptions down and get them signed off. Silent assumptions are where trust disappears later.

7.4 Describing the intervention

Boards do not need a treatise on models or prompts. They need a clear description of what will be different.

For each journey, state:

Scope

- Which customers, channels and intents are in scope.
- Any exclusions (e.g. high-risk segments that will remain human-only).

New operating model

- Which steps move to Green (AI can decide and act within policy).
- Which remain Amber (AI proposes; humans approve).
- Which stay Red (human-only decisions).

Expected shift in work mix

- Proportion of contacts expected to be fully AI-resolved.
- Proportion expected to be AI-prepared then human-resolved.
- Proportion remaining as traditional human handling.

Express this in simple tables rather than vague narratives. For example, for a journey:

Step	Before (who does what)	After (who does what)
Initial contact & explanation	Human-only, variable scripts	AI-first, human on escalation
Data gathering	Human asks, free-text notes	AI gathers in structured format
Option calculation	Human with calculator and policy notes	AI runs options within policy, human at edge cases
Agreement & confirmation	Human drafts, reads, records	AI drafts, human confirms in Amber/Red cases

The goal is that a non-technical board member can picture the new flow.

7.5 Costing the change

Costs should be:

- Complete enough to avoid surprises.
- Grouped simply enough to understand.

Think in four buckets:

1. **Design and build (one-off)**
    - Journey design and mapping.
    - Tooling and integrations.
    - Knowledge and guardrail work.
    - Testing, pilots and tuning.

2. **Technology (recurring)**

    - Platform, model and infrastructure costs.
    - Telephony, messaging and ancillary tooling where relevant.
    - Monitoring, logging and analytics.

3. **Operations (recurring)**

    - Run costs for AI-enabled journeys (e.g. AI platform + reduced human minutes).
    - New roles (journey owners, reviewers, content maintainers).
    - Additional QA and risk oversight.

4. **Change and enablement (one-off and early-phase)**

    - Training and communications.
    - Process and policy updates.
    - Temporary dual-running costs during cutover.

Make it clear what is:

- **Truly incremental** (new spend).
- **Reallocated** (e.g. some FTE shifting from frontline to QA or knowledge).

- **Offset** by stopping other work (e.g. retiring old systems or manual processes).

Avoid hiding costs in 'business as usual'. It is better to present a full picture and then discuss phasing than to be seen as minimising.

7.6 Modelling the benefits

Benefits fall into a few recurring categories:

Efficiency

- Reduced handling minutes per resolution.
- Lower CPR for targeted journeys.
- Reduced use of overtime, agency staff or outsourcing.

Capacity and resilience

- Ability to absorb peaks without the same cost or service degradation.
- Reduced queue times at critical periods.

Quality and risk

- Improved consistency of decision-making.
- Reduced error and complaint rates.
- Better vulnerability handling.

Revenue and value protection

- Higher cure rates in collections.
- Reduced churn in retention journeys.
- Higher conversion in sales journeys where applicable.

Do not try to monetise everything. Separate:

- **Hard benefits** you are willing to commit to the P&L.
- **Soft benefits** you will track but not bank upfront.

For example, you might commit to:

- A specific reduction in CPR for certain intents, based on a realistic forecast.
- A specific reduction in overtime spend given smoother peaks.

You might track, but not immediately bank, improvements in CSAT, NPS or staff engagement until you have data.

7.7 Using simple formulas and ranges

Boards do not need complex models; they need clarity and ranges.

At journey level:

- **CPR_before** = (total human minutes × cost per human minute) / resolutions
- **CPR_after** = (AI minutes × AI cost per minute + human minutes × cost per human minute) / resolutions

The **efficiency benefit per resolution** is:

- ΔCPR = CPR_before − CPR_after

Total annual efficiency benefit (if you choose to model it) is:

- Benefit = ΔCPR × expected number of resolutions per year

Do the same for any other hard benefits (e.g. changes in cure rates or churn) with formulas that can be explained on one slide.

Then apply a simple sensitivity:

Show the numbers if key drivers are **10% better than expected**, **as expected**, and **10% worse than expected**.

- Containment rate.
- AHT on escalated cases.
- Case volumes.

This avoids the impression that the case depends on a single, fragile point estimate.

7.8 Linking pilots to the business case

Pilots and proof-of-concept work often generate misleadingly good or bad results.

For pilots to support a business case:

Define pilot exit criteria upfront

- Operational (e.g. target containment, acceptable escalation and error rates).
- Risk (e.g. no material increase in complaints or specific error types).
- Experience (e.g. CSAT not worse than baseline).

Run pilots on representative traffic

- Not just hand-picked 'easy' queries.
- Not only during quiet periods.

Measure like-for-like

- Use the same definitions for AHT, containment, CPR and complaint rates before and during the pilot.
- Adjust for obvious differences in mix.

Translate pilot findings into cautious assumptions

- If a pilot shows a 30% improvement, you may choose to model 15–20% in the business case.
- Explain that you have applied a safety factor and why.

The pilot section of a business case should answer:

What did we test?

- On whom?

- For how long?
- What changed?
- What surprised us?
- What do we assume will generalise, and what will not?

This earns more trust than cherry-picked anecdotes.

7.9 Governance, RACI and decision gates

AI business cases should make governance explicit, not implied.

A simple RACI (Responsible, Accountable, Consulted, Informed) for each journey:

Accountable

- Journey owner (often in operations or a business unit).

Responsible

- Delivery lead (often in technology or a change function).
- Guardrail / policy owner (risk or compliance lead).
- Knowledge owner.

Consulted

- Legal, data protection, information security, frontline leadership, unions or staff forums where applicable.

Informed

- Executive sponsors, customer committees, risk committees.

Decision gates to surface:

Gate 0 – Intent selection

- Approval of journeys, segments and channels in scope.

Gate 1 – Design sign-off

- Agreement on RAG map, guardrails and target operating model.

Gate 2 – Pilot start

- Approval of pilot design, metrics, sampling and kill switch conditions.

Gate 3 – Pilot exit

- Decision to roll back, adjust or proceed to scaled deployment.

Gate 4 – Scale and embed

- Move into standard change governance, with regular performance and risk reviews.

Boards do not need to micromanage these gates, but they should see that they exist and are owned.

7.10 Common ways AI business cases go wrong

Recognising the failure modes upfront helps to avoid them. They tend to repeat. They might include:

Fantasy baselines

- No firm view of current volumes, AHT, CPR or complaint rates.
- Benefits calculated against imagined problems.

Over-claiming benefits

- Assuming very high containment, low error and no rework.
- Ignoring learning curves and change fatigue.

Ignoring rework and exception handling

- Not accounting for escalations and corrections when AI makes mistakes.
- Underestimating the effort needed to supervise and improve the system.

Thin view of risk and controls

- Treating risk as a section at the back, not integrated into design and costs.
- No clear evidence plan for regulators or auditors.

No reverse gear

- No costed plan to stop or roll back if the deployment is harmful or uneconomic.
- No clarity on who decides to use the kill switch and when.

No link to wider strategy

- AI projects not connected to broader goals for customer, digital or data strategy.
- Fragmented initiatives competing for the same people and systems.

A good business case calls these out explicitly and shows how they are being addressed.

7.11 Framing AI in the boardroom

How you **talk** about the case matters as much as the spreadsheets.

Useful framing:

- **This is a journey-level operational change, supported by AI**, not an 'AI project'.
- **We are starting small and safe**, with explicit guardrails and a reverse gear.
- **We are committing only to benefits we can sensibly measure and control.**
- **We will bring back evidence at defined gates**, and we have agreement on what 'good enough' looks like.

Unhelpful framing:

- 'Transformational AI'.
- Over-generalised claims about being 'left behind' without AI.
- Vendor language that does not match your architecture or risk posture.

- Hiding uncertainties instead of quantifying and containing them.

Boards are more likely to approve cases that feel measured, reversible and aligned with existing governance, not ones that sound like exceptions.

7.12 Setting up the optimisation story

A business case is not the end. It is the start of ongoing optimisation.

You will need to:

- Tune containment and escalation thresholds.
- Adjust guardrails as regulation, risk appetite and evidence change.
- Rebalance workloads across AI, humans and systems.
- Retire error classes over time.

The next chapter looks at optimisation and 'what's next': how to avoid locking yourself into a brittle design, and how to keep AI deployments aligned with reality as your operation and customer base change.

For now, the critical point is simple:

If you cannot explain your AI business case in a way that a non-technical board member understands and can defend, you are not ready to ask for their approval.

Takeaway. A credible business case is small, testable and reversible. It leads with outcomes and guardrails, shows arithmetic that anyone can re-run, binds itself to exit criteria, and reports weekly in a format that calms leaders. Do this and you will get approval faster, scale with fewer surprises, and avoid the ritual of over-promising followed by quiet backtracking.

Free board presentation document

If you would like to download our free board presentation document that you can use to engage your board with, copy and paste the URL below in to a browser:

https://forms.gle/QbiBmQPaEVkQwZCY7

Chapter 8

What's next for customer experience AI

In this Chapter we show how to keep improving without losing control.

Frameworks:

- *The danger of 'set and forget': drift, misalignment, decaying performance.*
- *Choosing what to optimise: trade-offs between cost, customer experience, risk, revenue.*
- *Simple optimisation loop: measure, diagnose, change, monitor.*
- *Calibration: keeping models aligned with reality using data and feedback.*
- *Three ways optimisation goes wrong: wrong objective, bad data, local over-optimisation.*
- *Tuning guardrails: adjusting risk appetite in controlled, observable ways.*
- *Improving human and AI together: joint coaching and feedback.*
- *Avoiding technology lock-in, clean interfaces, avoiding one-way doors.*

- *What 'next' looks like: signals of good practice and how this links back to early deployment and 90-day stories.*

8.1 The danger of 'set and forget'

The most expensive mistake you can make with AI in customer service is to treat go-live as the finish line.

Unlike a traditional IVR or a static script, an AI-enabled journey sits in the middle of moving parts:

- Policies and products change.
- Customer behaviour and expectations shift.
- Regulation evolves.
- Data quality drifts.
- Upstream and downstream systems are 'improved'.

If you do not actively monitor and tune, three things happen:

1. The system slowly diverges from reality.
2. People build workarounds that hide problems.
3. The business case quietly evaporates.

Optimisation is not a separate 'phase 2'. It is the operating model. This chapter is about making that model explicit.

8.2 Choosing what to optimise for

You cannot optimise for everything at once. If you do not choose, the optimiser (human or machine) will pick for you, usually in ways you do not like.

You should be able to state, for each journey:

"Our primary optimisation target is **X**, subject to **Y** and **Z** staying within defined bands."

Typical primary targets:

- **Containment** for self-serviceable, low-risk intents.
- **CPR (cost per resolution)** where efficiency is key, but quality and risk still matter.
- **Cure rate or churn reduction** for collections and retention journeys.
- **Time to reassurance** for emotionally heavy or high-stress journeys.

Typical constraints:

- Complaint rates must not rise above an agreed threshold.
- Specific error classes must stay below target levels.
- Vulnerability handling must meet defined standards.
- CSAT or other experience measures must not degrade materially.

If you simply say, "We want everything better," you hand control to whatever metric is easiest to move, usually at the expense of something you care about more but do not measure properly.

8.3 A simple optimisation loop

Forget grand language about 'closed-loop optimisation'. You need a loop that fits on one slide and can be run by mortals.

For each journey:

Set target & guardrails

- Choose primary target and constraints.
- Agree acceptable ranges with operations, risk and finance.

Measure and segment

- Gather performance data by: intent, segment, channel and time.
- Break down by: AI-resolved, AI-assisted and human-only.

Find tensions and anomalies

- Identify where improving one metric makes another worse.
- Spot unexpected shifts or outliers.

Hypothesise changes

Propose specific adjustments to:

- Guardrails and thresholds.
- Knowledge and prompts.

- Tools and routing.
- Escalation rules.

Test in controlled conditions

- Dark launch or limited traffic.
- Clear success and failure criteria.

Deploy or roll back

- Move changes into production if they pass.
- Roll back and document if they do not.

Review and log

- Record what you changed, why and what actually happened.
- Add to your playbook for that journey.

Repeat on a fixed rhythm (weekly or fortnightly), especially for high-volume journeys.

If you cannot show this loop in action, your AI is not being optimised; it is deteriorating.

8.4 Calibration: keeping models aligned with reality

Behind every metric is a model, explicit or implicit.

- A model of what 'affordable' means.

- A model of what counts as 'resolved'.
- A model of which signals indicate vulnerability.

These models are built into prompts, tools, thresholds and policies. They go stale.

Calibration is the routine of asking:

- "Is the system making roughly the same judgements a competent human would, given the same information?"
- "Do the numbers still match what we see on the ground?"

Practical calibration steps:

1. **Sample and compare**

- Take a representative set of cases.
- Have skilled humans review the AI's decisions or proposals.
- Record where they would agree, disagree, escalate or choose differently.

2. **Check label quality**

- Ensure intents, outcomes and error types are consistently recorded.
- If your labelling is noisy, your optimisation will be too.

3. **Align categories with business reality**

- Review error taxonomy and outcome codes periodically.
- Retire codes nobody uses; split overweight codes into more useful ones.

4. **Review thresholds**

- Affordability cut-offs.
- Risk scores for extra checks.
- Escalation thresholds for repeated contact or distress signals.

5. **Cross-check with external data**

- Complaints, external dispute decisions, audit findings.
- Where outside bodies disagree with you, update your models.

Calibration is not about tweaking prompts endlessly. It is about making sure the system's idea of 'acceptable behaviour' still matches your risk appetite and regulatory obligations.

8.5 Three ways optimisation goes wrong

Optimisation efforts tend to fail in a few predictable ways.

8.5.1 Optimising the wrong thing

Example:

- Driving containment up aggressively without watching repeat contact, complaints or downstream cost.

Symptoms:

- Dashboards look better.
- Frontline and complaints teams tell you things feel worse.

Fix:

- Re-state the objective with explicit constraints.
- Add missing metrics to the optimisation loop.
- Reverse changes that produce short-term numbers at long-term cost.

8.5.2 Optimising with bad data

Example:

- Using unreliable intent tags or inconsistent outcome codes as the basis for decisions.

Symptoms:

- Changes appear to help in dashboards but not in reality.
- Different teams produce conflicting analyses from the same data.

Fix:

- Invest in labelling quality: definitions, training, sampling and correction.
- Reduce the number of metrics and codes until you can trust them.
- Consider small, high-quality labelled sets for critical decisions.

8.5.3 Over-optimising locally

Example:

- Tweaking a single journey to look excellent while shifting complexity and cost into neighbouring journeys.

Symptoms:

- One team reports impressive improvements.
- Another team quietly absorbs extra work, risk or complaints.

Fix:

- Make the **unit of analysis** the end-to-end journey, not just a channel or team.
- Track handoffs and downstream interactions explicitly.
- Involve affected teams in optimisation discussions.

If you reward only local success, you will get local success and global mess.

8.6 Tuning guardrails without losing your nerve

Risk appetite is not fixed. It changes with:

- Economic conditions.
- Regulatory posture.
- Internal incidents and near-misses.
- Leadership changes.

You need a structured way to tune guardrails over time.

Approach:

Make guardrails parameterised

- Where possible, express limits as values you can change without rewriting everything (e.g. amounts, durations, thresholds).

Tie changes to evidence

For example:

- "We will expand Green scope for this step if, over three months, we see error rates below X and no increase in complaints Y and Z."
- "We will tighten this threshold if complaints on this category exceed A or regulators issue guidance B."

Run limited experiments

- Apply changes to a small segment (e.g. specific customer group or channel).
- Compare with a control group.

Document rationale

- Record why you changed a guardrail, what outcome you expected and what you actually saw.
- This matters for internal accountability and external scrutiny.

Guardrails that never move are unrealistic. Guardrails that move without trace are dangerous.

8.7 Improving human and AI together

Optimisation is not only about AI parameters. The human side can be tuned as well.

Areas to adjust:

Playbooks

- Simplify or clarify steps that consistently cause confusion or delay.
- Add or remove options based on observed outcomes.

Training and coaching

- Focus on areas where escalations are frequent or decisions inconsistent.
- Use real interactions where AI and humans disagreed as training material.

Role definitions

- Adjust who does what as the system stabilises.

- Move people towards more investigative, advisory or specialist work where volume allows.

Feedback channels

- Make it easy for frontline staff to flag patterns.
- Show them where their input led to specific changes.

The strongest indicator that your optimisation is working is when:

- Advisors feel the system is evolving in a direction that makes their work more effective and sustainable.
- Customers experience fewer friction points and dead ends.
- Risk teams see fewer nasty surprises and more small issues caught early.

8.8 Avoiding technology lock-in

Optimisation should strengthen your design, not tie you to particular tools forever.

To keep options open:

Design around journeys and patterns, not vendors.

- Your RAG maps, guardrails, knowledge and tools should not be specific to one provider's language.

Keep interfaces clear.

- Well-defined APIs and data contracts between systems.

- Separation between core logic (e.g. eligibility rules) and what a model is called.

Own your knowledge and guardrails.

- Policies, prompts, knowledge objects and runbooks should be documented and versioned in your environment, not locked in someone else's.

Benchmark occasionally.

- Test key journeys or tasks with alternative models or configurations, under controlled conditions.
- Use this to inform risk and cost decisions, not to chase trends.

If you cannot change or re-platform parts of your stack without unpicking everything, you have built an AI monolith. Those do not age well.

8.9 What 'next' actually looks like

Predictions about the future of AI in customer service tend to oscillate between two extremes:

- Everything becomes fully automated.
- Nothing really changes and agents 'remain central'.

Reality will be duller and more useful.

Likely trends:

More journeys, not fewer

- Once you have a robust pattern for a few journeys, it will be applied across more of your operation.
- The constraint shifts from technology to the speed at which you can safely change policies, tools and training.

Finer-grained segmentation

- You will not treat all customers the same.
- Different risk appetites and service levels will emerge for different segments and contexts.

Richer tools

- More actions will be exposed as tools, enabling deeper automation where safe.
- Internal systems will be refactored around journeys, not departments.

Tighter integration with upstream and downstream processes

- AI in service will influence, and be influenced by, product design, pricing, marketing and collections strategies.
- Feedback loops will shorten.

Higher expectations of evidence

- Regulators and partners will expect clearer explanations of how decisions are made and controlled.

- 'We used an AI' will not count as a defence.

Changing skills mix

- Fewer people doing repetitive, scripted work.
- More people doing case handling, design, analysis, governance and coaching.

Nothing about this requires speculation about general intelligence. It is an extension of the patterns already covered in this book.

8.10 Signals that you are doing it well

You do not need a grand maturity model. You can ask a few blunt questions instead.

If you are doing this well:

- You can list the journeys where AI is live, with named owners and clear RAG maps.
- You can show monthly performance packs for those journeys that mix economics, quality, risk and experience.
- You have changed guardrails at least once, based on evidence, and can show before/after effects.
- Frontline staff can explain, in their own words, what the assistant does, what it does not do, and how to escalate.
- Risk and legal teams can pull samples and trace decisions without weeks of archaeology.

- You can point to specific error classes that have been eliminated or materially reduced.

If you cannot do these things, you are still at the experimental stage, however sophisticated the technology looks.

8.11 Connecting back to the 90-day plan

Optimisation is not something you start in year two. It is baked into how you approach the first 90 days.

From the 90-day plan in the conclusion:

- The **baselining work** becomes your benchmark for optimisation.
- The **guardrails and RAG decisions** become your first set of parameters to tune.
- The **pilot metrics and error taxonomy** become the backbone of your optimisation loop.
- The **squad and governance structure** become the forum in which changes are proposed, tested and approved.

The point of this chapter is not to make optimisation sound exotic. It is to normalise it:

AI-enabled journeys are never ‘done’. They are either being actively maintained and improved, or they are drifting.

The conclusion ties this together, focusing on how to lead the next 90 days in a way that sets you up for years rather than quarters.

Takeaway. The next wave won’t look like science fiction. It will look like shorter paths, steadier numbers, kinder escalations and fewer surprises. Do the small, boring things with discipline and the impressive bits will follow. Customers will describe your service as ‘easy’. Boards will approve faster. Regulators will nod more. That's the real future: less drama, more finish.

Conclusion

Leading through the next 90 days

C.1 This is not about 'AI projects'

If you strip away the slides, the vendor language and the headlines, this book has really been about three things:

- Designing **better journeys** for customers and staff.
- Deciding **who does what** between AI, humans and systems.
- Keeping everything **inside guardrails** you can defend.

AI did not change what customers want: they want clear outcomes, minimal effort, honesty when things go wrong.

AI changed what is possible:

- You can handle more concurrent conversations without collapsing service.
- You can apply policy more consistently under pressure.
- You can see and improve work with better data.

What matters now is not what you believe about AI in the abstract. It is what you do in the next 90 days.

C.2 The leadership challenge

As a leader, you own three questions:

1. **Where do we start, specifically?**
2. **How do we move fast without losing control?**
3. **How do we bring people and risk with us, not drag them behind?**

You do not need a ten-year roadmap to answer these. You need a disciplined 90-day plan that:

- Starts small and concrete.
- Builds trust through evidence.
- Leaves you with something live, measurable and adjustable.

The rest of this conclusion is that plan.

C.3 The 90-day plan at a glance

A simple way to think about the next three months:

Period	Focus	Question answered
Days 1–10	Choose & understand	'Where exactly will we start?'
Days 11–30	Design & guardrail	'What will we allow this thing to do?'
Days 31–60	Build, pilot & learn	'Does this actually work in our world?'
Days 61–90	Scale safely & embed	'How do we make this part of how we operate?'

Each phase has concrete actions and artefacts. By the end of Day 90, you should have:

- One or two journeys live with AI and humans working together.
- Guardrails and RAG maps you can explain to risk, regulators and staff.
- A basic optimisation loop in place.
- Enough evidence to decide what to do next, with more confidence and less noise.

C.4 Days 1–10: choose and understand

Goal: Agree where to start and how bad 'today' really is.

Actions:

1. **Name one or two journeys**

Pick high-volume, repeatable, structurally similar work where:

- Customers currently have a poor or inconsistent experience.
- Staff deal with the same patterns over and over.
- Risk is present but manageable.

Examples: missed payments, broken product journeys, simple technical faults, change of address.

2. **Form a small cross-functional squad**

- Operations (journey owner).

- Frontline representation.
- Risk/compliance.
- Technology / architecture.
- Data / MI.
- Someone who actually writes things: knowledge or content owner.

3. **Map the 'as-is' journey end-to-end**

- Use a simple table: steps, customer intent, systems touched, who does what, failure points.
- Identify where customers repeat themselves, where staff improvise and where risk is highest.

4. **Baseline the current state**

For each selected journey:

- Volumes and seasonality.
- Containment, FCR, AHT, CPR, complaints.
- Any existing vulnerability or risk flags.

Capture assumptions explicitly where data is thin.

Artefacts by Day 10

- A short note: *"We are starting with these journeys, for these reasons."*
- As-is journey maps, agreed by the squad.

- A baseline pack you are not embarrassed to show finance and risk.

C.5 Days 11–30: design and guardrail

Goal: Decide what 'good' looks like and what the AI will and will not do.

Actions:

1. **Define the target operating model for each journey**

- Apply the RAG model to each step: Green, Amber, Red.
- Decide which steps are AI-first, which are AI-assisted human, which stay human-only.
- Write this in a format a frontline advisor could repeat back.

2. **Write the purpose and scope note**

For each assistant or journey, document in one page:

- Purpose: what it is for.
- Out of scope: what it will never do.
- Supported journeys and steps (with RAG).
- Channels and segments in scope.

3. **Draft the guardrail stack**

- Disclosure: how you will tell customers they are speaking to an 'Assistant' and what their options are.
- Identity & access: verification levels, channel rules, acting-for-others.
- Data & retention: what is collected, how it is stored, how long you keep it.
- Language & vulnerability: tone, prohibited behaviours, escalation triggers.
- Payments & money: secure flows, affordability steps, limits on offers.
- Logging & audit: what will be logged and how it will be sampled.
- Kill switch & rollback: conditions under which you stop the system and how.

4. **Involve risk, legal and compliance properly**

- Share purpose, scope, guardrails and RAG maps.
- Ask them to mark red lines and open questions.
- Agree what evidence they will want to see during pilots.

5. **Engage frontline leaders**

- Explain what will change in their world, not 'AI in general'.
- Describe the mix shift: which contacts will reduce, which will increase, and what new support they will have.
- Confirm there will be a shadow/training period before fully going-live.

Artefacts by Day 30:

- RAG maps and target operating models per journey.
- Purpose & scope note for each assistant.
- Draft guardrail stack, with comments and input from risk/compliance.
- Agreement on what a 'safe' pilot looks like and how you will stop it if needed.

C.6 Days 31–60: build, pilot and learn

Goal: Prove that the redesigned journey works for real customers under real conditions.

Actions:

1. **Build the minimum viable journey**

- Tools: create or refine the API calls and write-paths needed to resolve the journey safely.

- Knowledge: write and lock golden answers where wording matters, with owners and review dates.
- Orchestration: implement the seven-step agentic loop (Listen, Plan, Retrieve, Act, Check, Summarise, Decide) for each in-scope step.
- Interfaces: ensure advisors can see, override and correct what the assistant does.

2. **Set up logging and MI**

- Log: who, what, when, tools used, knowledge versions, outcomes, escalations, errors.

Build simple dashboards for:

- Volumes and mix (AI-resolved, AI-assisted, human-only).
- Containment, AHT, CPR, CSAT where available.
- Error types and complaint rates.

3. **Run a shadow mode period**

- Let the assistant observe and propose responses without sending them.
- Ask advisors to rate proposals (would send/would edit/unsafe).
- Use this to refine prompts, knowledge and tools.

4. **Run a limited pilot**

- Turn the assistant on for a small, well-defined portion of traffic (e.g. one channel, one segment, certain hours).
- Keep kill switches live and clear.
- Sample interactions for quality and safety; classify errors with a small taxonomy.

5. **Hold regular pilot reviews**

Weekly or fortnightly:

- What is working as expected?
- What is worse than expected?
- What surprised us?

Decide what to:

- Fix immediately.
- Accept with monitoring.
- Block or roll back.

Artefacts by Day 60:

- A working, AI-enabled journey in pilot with real customers.
- MI showing before/after comparisons for key metrics.
- A small but real error taxonomy with owners for each class.
- A list of changes already made based on evidence.

C.7 Days 61–90: scale safely and embed

Goal: Move from pilot to something you can call part of the operation without crossing your fingers.

Actions:

1. **Decide on scale-up, pause or rollback**

- Use the criteria you agreed earlier with operations, risk and finance.

For each journey, ask:

- Are the benefits real and stable?
- Are the risks understood and controlled?
- Do frontline teams feel we are moving in the right direction?

2. **Extend scope stepwise**

- Increase traffic share, channels, or segments deliberately rather than all at once.

After each extension, re-check:

- Containment, AHT, CPR, complaints, vulnerability handling.

3. **Embed governance**

- Confirm journey owners and cross-functional squads for ongoing optimisation.

- Set a standing review rhythm: monthly performance and risk review per journey, with a simple optimisation loop.
- Align change control: no untracked changes to tools, knowledge or guardrails.

4. **Reset performance management**

- Adjust metrics and targets for advisors whose work mix has shifted.
- Avoid holding them to old AHT expectations when they are now handling more complex, emotionally heavy cases.
- Add quality, risk and improvement contributions into how you judge performance.

5. **Communicate honestly and repeatedly**

To staff:

- What we have learned.
- What is changing next.
- Where AI has helped, and where it has not.

To risk and legal:

- Evidence on outcomes, error profiles, complaints and incidents.

To senior leadership and boards:

- Results against the business case.

- Updated view of where to invest next.

Artefacts by Day 90:

- At least one AI-enabled journey running as part of normal operations.
- A basic but working optimisation process (data, review, change, re-measure).
- Clear allocation of responsibilities and decision rights.
- A refreshed roadmap for the next set of journeys based on what you have actually learned.

C.8 What to do if you stall

You will stall somewhere. The point is not to avoid stall; it is to recognise and deal with it quickly.

Common sticking points:

1. **Data and baselines are weak**
   - **Symptom**: endless argument about how bad 'today' really is.
   - **Response**: pick a reasonable baseline using sampling and agreed assumptions; mark it clearly and move. Perfection is not coming any time soon.
2. **Guardrail debates drag on**
   - **Symptom**: risk and operations cannot agree on boundaries.
   - **Response**: start with a more conservative scope (more Amber and Red), then agree on evidence required to move specific steps towards Green.

3. **Frontline resistance hardens**

    - **Symptom**: advisors feel changes are 'done to' them and quietly undermine adoption.
    - **Response**: tighten the feedback loop. Put real examples of changes driven by their input on the wall. Fix at least one painful issue fast, visibly, because they raised it.

4. **Technology complexity overwhelms**

    - **Symptom**: integration, legacy systems or vendor negotiations soak up all energy.
    - **Response**: narrow scope further. Prioritise journeys where existing tools are sufficient. You are not rebuilding the entire estate in 90 days.

5. **Leadership attention moves on**

    - **Symptom**: initiative becomes 'the AI project' owned by a single function.
    - **Response**: bring it back to journeys, economics and risk. Remind people this is about how you serve customers and control cost, not about a technology toy.

If you cannot unstick a specific journey, the safest option is to pause it, capture what you learned and start with another journey that is more tractable. Evidence does not go to waste.

C.9 How to know you are on the right track

You are probably on the right track if:

- You can name the journeys where AI is live, and also name the journey owners.

- Frontline staff can describe what the assistant does and does not do, and how to escalate.

- Risk, legal and compliance can access logs and MI without a special project.

- You have changed at least one guardrail or threshold based on evidence, not opinion.

- You can point to a specific error class or failure pattern that has been materially reduced.

- You can show that for at least one journey, CPR has improved or service resilience has increased without a rise in serious complaints.

You are probably not on the right track if:

- 'AI' lives in innovation decks but not in MI packs.

- Nobody can say which journeys are in scope.

- Frontline staff describe AI as 'that thing that makes my life harder'.

- Risk has effectively blocked all deployments because they do not trust the controls.

- The only benefits discussed are hypothetical.

You do not need perfection. You need honest progress and a system that gets a little better each month, not just at quarter-end presentations.

C.10 A final note on leadership

The organisations that will get the most from AI in customer service are not the ones with the most sophisticated models. They are the ones with leaders who:

- Treat AI as part of operations, not a separate spectacle.
- Are prepared to say 'no' to reckless use cases, even when they are fashionable.
- Are equally prepared to push past inertia where the risks are manageable and the benefits clear.
- Are willing to learn enough about the technology to ask good questions, but not so much that they forget the point is serving customers and protecting the business.

You do not have to be an expert in models. You do have to be serious about journeys, guardrails and evidence.

The next 90 days will not 'transform' your customer service. If they go well, they will do something more valuable and less dramatic:

- Prove, in your own estate, that AI can be used safely and usefully.
- Give your teams a working pattern they can reuse.
- Move you from talking about AI to operating with it.

After that, the work is simply more of the same: one journey at a time, one error class at a time, one guardrail adjustment at a time, until 'AI in customer service' is no longer a project at all. It is just how you run the place.

Method Note

How to read and apply this book

Purpose

Give senior leaders and operators a **portable operating system** for agentic AI and AI voice agents in customer service: precise definitions, minimal metrics, repeatable artefacts (guardrails, knowledge discipline, exit criteria), and small pieces of arithmetic that hold up in front of boards and regulators.

Scope and stance

- **Audience:** directors, operations, product, compliance, data and security.
- **Voice:** plain UK English; short sentences; no vendor jargon.
- **Evidence:** baselines, typed errors, versioned knowledge, reproducible CPR maths, ±10% sensitivities.
- **Ethos:** short plans, strong fences, honest numbers.

Definitions used consistently

- **Intent:** what the customer wants to achieve, with a clear 'done' state.

- **Containment:** share of scoped interactions resolved without a human.
- **AHT (Average Handle Time):** AI + human + waiting minutes to resolution.
- **CPR (Cost per Resolution):** handling cost per successful resolution.
- **VPR (Value per Resolution):** attributable £ uplift per resolution where relevant.
- **Latency p95:** slow-tail performance the customer feels.
- **Golden answers:** approved, locked wording for regulated/risk-bearing statements.
- **Do-not-automate zones:** policy-defined areas reserved for humans.
- **Handoff packet:** short context sent to advisors on escalation.

Worked arithmetic (one-liners)

Human-only CPR = $m_h \times c_h$

AI-first CPR = $m_{ai} \times c_{ai} + (1 - containment) \times m_{h,esc} \times c_h$

Blended CPR = $containment \times (m_{ai} \times c_{ai}) + (1 - containment) \times (m_{ai,assist} \times c_{ai} + m_{h,assist} \times c_h)$

Monthly cost = $volume \times CPR \times resolution\_rate$

Sensitivity: vary **containment** and **escalated minutes** by **±10%** to produce `sensitivity_low/high_gbp`.

Choosing intents

Start where **write-paths** exist, outcomes are clear, and knowledge is owned: status checks, simple changes, secure-link payments, structured intakes.

Flow standards

Outcome first. Identity once. Small plans. Confirm writes. Summarise. Gracefully stop and escalate on ambiguity, distress, missing write-paths or identity doubt.

Evaluation rhythm

Shadow → limited live 10–20% → weekly calibration (one-page metrics + five transcripts) → exit criteria → scale.

Exit criteria (minimum)

Containment at target; CPR below baseline; complaints no worse; disclosure ≥ 99%; zero severity-one incidents for 14 days; guardrails and knowledge artefacts up to date; rollback rehearsal passed.

Numbers discipline

Round visibly; separate enablement from run-rate; never count read-only as resolution; state redeployment assumptions when you claim capacity benefits.

Language discipline

Expand acronyms on first use in each major section, then use the acronym consistently. Prefer ordinary microcopy to legalese or theatrical marketing.

Data & Reporting Schema

Purpose

Provide a **minimal field dictionary** and four stable reporting views that produce consistent, comparable, decision-grade reporting across operations, compliance and the board. The schema favours **small, high-signal fields** over exhaust, and stores **status and references**, not raw payloads.

Core table: `interactions`

Represents a single customer interaction end to end, across channels and actors.

Field	Type	Notes
`interaction_id`	string	Unique ID for traceability.
`customer_internal_id_hash`	string	Hashed; avoid raw identifiers in analytics.
`intent_code`	string	Canonical code from the intent catalogue.
`channel`	enum	voice, chat, email, form, social.
`start_ts` / `end_ts`	timestamp	UTC; compute duration from these.
`resolved_flag`	bool	True only if 'done' state met in system of record.

`escalated_flag`	bool	True if handed to a human advisor.
`ai_minutes`	decimal	Assistant handling time.
`human_minutes`	decimal	Advisor handling time.
`pathway`	enum	ai_first, blended, human_only.
`identity_verified_flag`	bool	Whether identity was verified.
`identity_method`	enum	otp, in_app, known_device, kba, none.
`disclosure_given_flag`	bool	Proof of opening disclosure.
`payment_link_used_flag`	bool	Payments via link/hosted page only.
`do_not_record_segment_flag`	bool	Whether a non-recorded segment occurred.
`complaint_flag`	bool	Y/N during or immediately after interaction.
`opt_out_flag`	bool	Customer opted out of automation/marketi ng.
`error_type`	enum	Typed error taxonomy (see below).
`resolution_value_gbp`	decimal	Optional; for collections/saves.

Derived:

- `aht_minutes` = `ai_minutes + human_minutes + waiting_minutes` (if tracked).
- `pathway_cpr_gbp` (see CPR formulae below).

Core table: `knowledge_versions`

Versioned catalogue for answers and policies.

Field	Type	Notes
`kv_id`	string	Knowledge item identifier.
`topic`	string	Human-readable title.
`owner`	string	Named person/role.
`version`	string	Semantic versioning, e.g., 3.4.
`approved_ts`	timestamp	Approval time.
`next_review_due`	date	Mandatory to avoid staleness.
`regulated_flag`	bool	Triggers golden-answer controls.
`golden_answer_hash`	string	Integrity check for locked copy.

Core table: `guardrails`

The live rulebook.

Field	Type	Notes
`guardrail_id`	string	Unique ID.
`category`	enum	disclosure, identity, lawful_basis, do_not_automate, payments, language_limits, rollback.
`version`	string	Version of the guardrail set.
`owner`	string	Named person/role.
`effective_ts`	timestamp	Start of validity.
`summary`	string	Plain-English description.

Core table: `benefits_tracker_weekly`

The single page leaders read.

Field	Type	Notes
week_commencing	date	ISO week start.
intent_code	string	From catalogue.
volume	integer	Count of interactions.
containment_pct	decimal	% resolved by AI.
aht_minutes	decimal	Whole-path AHT.
cpr_gbp	decimal	Cost per resolution.
latency_p50_seconds	integer	Median latency.
latency_p95_seconds	integer	Peak pain.
complaint_rate_pct	decimal	Per 100 interactions.
opt_out_rate_pct	decimal	Per 100 interactions.
top_error_type	enum	From taxonomy.
fix_shipped	bool	Whether a mitigation shipped.
owner	string	Accountable person.
cash_delta_gbp	decimal	vs baseline.
sensitivity_low/high_gbp	decimal	±10% driver range.

Typed error taxonomy (12 classes)

Short, actionable, and sufficient for weekly retirement cadence:

1. identity_doubt
2. knowledge_stale
3. policy_ambiguous
4. disclosure_missing
5. tool_timeout
6. no_write_path
7. unsafe_language
8. looping_prompts
9. handoff_missing_context
10. payment_link_issue
11. do_not_record_misuse
12. accessibility_failure

CPR and cost formulae (one-liners)

Human-only CPR = $m_h \times c_h$

AI-first CPR = $m_{ai} \times c_{ai} + (1 - containment) \times m_{h,esc} \times c_h$

Blended CPR = $containment \times (m_{ai} \times c_{ai}) + (1 - containment) \times (m_{ai,assist} \times c_{ai} + m_{h,assist} \times c_h)$

Monthly cost = $volume \times CPR \times resolution\_rate$

Sensitivity: vary **containment** and **escalated minutes** by **±10%** to produce `sensitivity_low/high_gbp`.

Minimal dashboards (four stable views)

1. Experience

- Containment % by intent
- Latency p50/p95
- Complaint rate %
- Opt-out rate %

2. Economics

- AHT minutes
- CPR £
- Cash delta vs baseline
- Sensitivity range

3. **Quality & Safety**

- Disclosure %
- Identity %
- Do-not-record compliance
- Error classes retired this week

4. **Reliability**

- Dependency timeouts
- Tool success rates
- Feature-flag status (per intent)

Each view fits on one page. Add a **6–8 sentence change note**: what shipped, what moved, what's next.

Field guidance and retention

- **Identity:** store **status** and **method**, not secrets.
- **Payments:** store **link issuance** and **state**, never card data.
- **Analytics:** store **references and states**; redact free text.
- **Residency:** record processor and location; prefer UK/EU where policy demands.
- **Retention:** short, policy-aligned periods; scheduled deletion jobs with logs.

Intent catalogue (minimum viable)

intent_code	name	done_state	owner
`status.order`	Order status	Confirmed ETA or completion	Ops lead
`change.address`	Address update	Address written to CRM with confirmation	Ops lead
`billing.pay_now`	One-off payment	Link issued, payment success recorded	Finance lead
`billing.dd_setup`	Direct debit setup	Mandate created and verified	Finance lead
`access.reset`	Password reset	Reset confirmed, next login guidance sent	Security lead
`policy.explain_fee`	Fee explanatio n	Explanation delivered; acceptance or escalation	Compliance lead
`complaint.intake`	Complaint intake	Case created, SLA timer started	Complaints lead
`care.hardship`	Hardship flag	Escalated with context; owner assigned	Vulnerability lead

Handoff context packet (standard fields)

Field	Notes
Identity status/method/timestamp	So advisors don't repeat verification.
Goal (customer's words)	Plain English, short.
Steps attempted	With tool names and outcomes.
Artefacts captured	Files/photos and where they live.
Next sensible action	One line.
Time constraints	SLAs, pending timers.

Reporting cadence

- **Daily:** quick numbers scan; investigate outliers.
- **Weekly:** publish benefits tracker; retire or mitigate one error class.
- **Monthly:** guardrail and knowledge review; rollback rehearsal.
- **Quarterly:** portfolio update (add/retire intents based on volume, CPR and feasibility).

Takeaway. Keep data small and decisive. Store states, not secrets. Report in four views with one short narrative. Tie every typed error to an owner and retire one class per week. That is enough to steer a modern, compliant, agentic service.

Appendices

Appendix A

Guardrails template (operational rulebook)

Purpose: A short, versioned rulebook the assistant enforces and people recognise.

Version: GRD-1.0 • Owner: Product/Compliance • Effective: [date]

A1. Disclosure

- Opening sentence: "I'm an automated assistant. I can complete most requests, and you can speak to a person at any time."
- Re-disclose on channel switches and at handoff.
- `KPI: disclosure ≥ 99.0%.`

A2. Identity

- Methods: one-time code (OTP), in-app confirm, known device. Knowledge-based answers (KBA) discouraged.
- Rule: verify once; carry status; step up only for high-risk actions (e.g., bank details change).
- Log: `verified:Y/N`, `method`, `timestamp`.

A3. Lawful basis and consent

Map per intent/step: contract, legitimate interest, legal obligation, consent.

Keep copy short, link to privacy notice. Honour customer opt-out immediately.

A4. Do-not-automate zones

- Redress decisions, hardship determinations, clinical/legal advice, discretionary waivers beyond policy, explicit regulator-reserved steps.

A5. Payments

- Only via verified link or hosted page. No in-channel card capture.
- Store issuance/state; never store PAN/CVV.

A6. Language limits

- Reading age target 10–12; no claims that exceed policy; accessible alternatives available on request.

A7. Rollback and stop conditions

- Stop on: identity doubt, policy ambiguity, missing write-path, distress signals, customer requests a human.
- Rollback: feature flags per intent; reversals documented and rehearsed monthly.

A8. Release rhythm

- Dark launch → canary → limited live. No Friday launches. Monthly rollback drill.

Appendix B

DPIA (Data Protection Impact Assessment) one-pager

Project: Agentic assistant for [intents] • Owner: DPO • Version: DPIA-0.9

1. **Purpose & lawful basis:** per intent/step, short line each.
2. **Data map:** categories, sources, processors, residency (UK/EU), retention.
3. **Risks:** accuracy, policy, privacy, security, fairness/accessibility.
4. **Controls:** disclosure, identity-once, do-not-automate, payments by link, audit trail, feature flags, rollback rehearsal.
5. **Mitigations → checks:** each control tied to a test/monitor.
6. **Residual risk & sign-off:** owner, acceptance, review date.

Appendix C

Benefits tracker (board-ready)

Template fields (weekly, per intent):

- Week commencing | Volume | Containment % | AHT mins (whole path) | CPR £ | Latency p50/p95 s | Complaint % | Opt-out % | Top error class | Fix shipped (Y/N) | Owner | Cash delta £ | Sensitivity low/high £

Narrative footer (6–8 lines): what shipped, what moved, top risk, next week's fix.

Appendix D

Pilot exit criteria pack

Scope: 2–3 resolvable intents with live write-paths.

Must hit within 4–8 weeks:

- Containment ≥ [target range].
- CPR below baseline by [x–y] £ with ±10% sensitivity shown.
- Complaint/opt-out no worse than baseline.
- Disclosure ≥ 99%; identity at policy %.
- Zero Sev-1 incidents over last 14 days.
- Guardrails/knowledge current; rollback drill passed this month.

Decision: scale / hold / stop, with reasons and actions.

Appendix E

Handoff context packet (advisor view)

Fields:

- Identity: verified Y/N, method, timestamp
- Customer goal (verbatim)
- Steps attempted + results (with references)
- Artefacts captured (where stored)
- Next sensible action
- Time constraints/SLA

Advisor two-sentence restart (pattern): acknowledge progress, confirm goal, state immediate next step.

Appendix F

Microcopy standards

Principles: short, concrete, neutral; choices with consequences; honest limits; proof of finish.

Examples:

- Confirmation: "I've updated your address to 12 Poynton Road, M20 6AB, effective today."
- Choices: "Move to the 1st or 15th; your direct debit date changes accordingly."
- Boundary: "I can't decide hardship outcomes. I'll bring a colleague in now."
- Proof: "Reference A1B2C3, updated 14:03 today."

Process: versioned catalogue; golden answers locked for regulated statements; review dates scheduled.

Appendix G

Golden answers operating procedure

When to lock: regulated wording, fees, determinations, eligibility statements, privacy text.

Fields: topic, version, owner, next review, hash, locale variants.

Usage rule: 'Assistant' must prefer golden answers over generative phrasing; internal logs cite version.

Appendix H

Rollback rehearsal script

Cadence: monthly, 30 minutes.

1. **Trigger**: simulate tool timeout or disclosure regression on one intent.
2. **Contain**: flip feature flag to 0% for affected intent.
3. **Communicate**: internal banner to advisors; short customer copy if impact user-visible.
4. **Recover**: revert change; confirm state in system of record; close references.
5. **Learn**: update guardrail or test; log rehearsal completion.

Appendix I

Accessibility checklist (minimum viable)

- Readable copy and examples; jargon removed or explained.
- Alt text and captions; transcripts for audio; pace control for voice.
- Low-bandwidth fallback for forms and status checks.
- Locale-aware golden answers reviewed by domain experts.
- Do-not-record segments clearly indicated where policy demands.

Appendix J

Outbound compliance aide-mémoire

- Lawful basis: consent where required; otherwise documented legitimate-interest test; honour objections immediately.
- Disclosure: who, why, and how to reach a person now.
- Evidence: include enough detail to act without searching old messages.
- Choice: human route present; one-tap opt-out persists across channels.
- Records: purpose, basis, opt-out state, copy version.

Appendix K

Typed error taxonomy and cadence

Twelve classes: identity_doubt; knowledge_stale; policy_ambiguous; disclosure_missing; tool_timeout; no_write_path; unsafe_language; looping_prompts; handoff_missing_context; payment_link_issue; do_not_record_misuse; accessibility_failure.

Weekly target: retire or mitigate one class; owner and date visible in tracker.

Appendix L

Intent selection rubric

Score = Volume × CPR delta × Feasibility (1–5 each)

- Volume: monthly interactions
- CPR delta: £ reduction potential
- Feasibility: write-paths, policy clarity, knowledge maturity, customer tolerance

Pick the top 2–3; ignore fashionable but fragile intents.

Appendix M

Data minimisation patterns

- Store states and references; avoid raw payloads in analytics.
- Record identity **status/method**, not secrets.
- Payments: record **link issuance/state** only.
- Redact free text; set deletion jobs to run on schedule.

Appendix N

Reporting views (layout spec)

Experience: containment, p95, complaint/opt-out.

Economics: AHT, CPR, cash delta, sensitivity range.

Quality & Safety: disclosure %, identity %, do-not-record compliance, error classes retired.

Reliability: dependency timeouts, tool success, feature-flag status.

Each view fits a page with uniform axes and stable ordering.

Appendix O

Weekly calibration agenda (20 minutes)

- Numbers: 5 mins (move/not move).
- Five transcripts: 10 mins (two wins, three issues).
- Decision: 3 mins (one error class to retire).
- Owners/next steps: 2 mins.

Ship one microcopy or guardrail fix immediately where safe.

Appendix P

Partner vs DIY comparison (decision aid)

Criterion	DIY	Specialist partner
Time to value	Longer; assemble stack, design artefacts	Faster; artefacts and cadence pre-built
Control evidence	Must be invented	Guardrails, golden answers, DPIA, rollback drilled
Reporting	Patchy, delayed	Real-time, intent-level, sensitivity shown
Risk	Higher until habits form	Lower via repeatable controls
Cost curve	Lumpy up-front	Smoother, linked to outcomes

Use once; then decide with eyes open.

Appendices takeaway: Use these artefacts as working documents, not shelfware. Keep them short, versioned and visible. Tie every weekly improvement to one of them so progress compounds.

Glossary

Access control Technical and process controls that restrict who can view or change data or systems, typically enforced through roles and permissions.

Accessibility The design of products and services so people with disabilities can use them, including alternatives for low vision/hearing and low bandwidth.

Accuracy (data protection principle) The requirement under data-protection law to keep personal data accurate and up to date, with reasonable steps to correct inaccuracies.

AI (Artificial Intelligence) Computer systems that perform tasks requiring human-like perception, reasoning or language skills. In this book, AI is used to recognise intents, retrieve knowledge, plan small steps and execute authorised actions.

AI voice agent An AI service 'Assistant' that speaks on your phone lines, using speech recognition and text to speech to run the same journeys, tools and rulebook as a text-based assistant. In this book, AI voice agents are treated as first class citizens alongside human advisors.

AHT (Average Handle Time) Total minutes across the whole path to resolution, including assistant minutes, human minutes and waiting. Used in CPR calculation.

Ambiguity (policy) A state where two or more policies conflict or a rule requires judgement beyond automation. Triggers a stop condition and escalation.

Append-only logging Audit logging pattern where records are written but never edited, supporting trustworthy hindsight trails.

API (Application Programming Interface) A structured way for software to talk to software. In this book, tools use APIs to read/write to systems of record.

Audit trail Human-readable record of inputs, versions, actions, outcomes and decisions that explains what happened and why.

Authentication Proving a user is who they claim to be, e.g., one-time passcodes, in-app confirmations, known devices.

Authorisation Granting a verified user permission to do specific things, usually enforced by roles.

Baseline Pre-pilot measurement of volume, AHT, CPR, latency, complaints and opt-outs used to compare performance during and after deployment.

Benefits tracker Weekly, one-page report by intent: volume, containment, AHT, CPR, latency, complaint/opt-out, top error class, fix shipped, owner, cash delta, sensitivity range.

Blended model Operations where AI and humans work together: AI handles recognition/retrieval/routine writes; humans handle judgement, empathy, negotiation and finishing.

Board pack Two-page decision summary plus annex (guardrails, DPIA, benefits tracker, incident/rollback records) used for approvals.

Calibration Short weekly session that reviews one page of numbers and five transcripts, selects one typed error class to retire, and ships one fix.

Capacity The volume of interactions an operation can handle at acceptable latency and quality. Improved by AI concurrency and shorter human minutes.

Cardholder data Payment card information that must not be handled in-channel by the assistant. Use payment links/hosted forms instead.

CDR (Call Detail Record) Telephony metadata. Not a substitute for a human-readable audit trail of agentic decisions.

CFR (Closed-Form Resolution) Outcome with a clear system-of-record change and confirmation reference.

Change control Process that schedules, tests, releases and can roll back changes. Uses feature flags, canary traffic and rehearsed reversal.

Channel The medium used by the customer (voice, chat, email, forms, social). Channels are pipes; outcomes happen in systems of record.

Complaint (formal) An expression of dissatisfaction requiring acknowledgement and possible redress under sector rules. Intake can be automated; determination is generally human.

Concurrency The ability to handle many interactions in parallel at low marginal cost. A major AI advantage.

Confidence (model) A measure of certainty used to decide whether to proceed, clarify or escalate. Low confidence triggers stop conditions.

Containment Percentage of scoped interactions resolved end-to-end by AI without a human. Always paired with quality and CPR.

Context packet The handoff bundle for advisors: identity status/method, goal in the customer's words, steps attempted, results and references, artefacts captured, next sensible action, time constraints.

CPR (Cost per Resolution) Handling minutes × unit cost across the whole path (AI + human + waiting). Core economic measure.

CSR (Customer Service Representative) Human advisor. In this book, the person who finishes work requiring judgement or discretion.

Data minimisation Collecting and processing only the minimum data needed for the stated purpose; a UK GDPR principle.

DPA 2018 (Data Protection Act 2018) UK legislation implementing and supplementing UK GDPR. Sets obligations and rights for processing personal data.

DPIA (Data Protection Impact Assessment) A structured assessment of privacy risks and mitigations for high-risk processing. In this book, a live map tied to checks and monitoring.

Do-not-automate zone A policy boundary reserving certain decisions or steps for trained humans (e.g., hardship determinations, redress outcomes, clinical/legal advice).

Do-not-record segment A short, explicitly marked part of an interaction where recording is paused for policy or legal reasons, followed by clear re-entry into recorded service.

Edge (computing) Executing small checks (identity pings, eligibility reads) closer to the customer to reduce latency or keep data local.

Eligibility check Deterministic rule gate that must pass before an action can proceed (e.g., tariff switch rules).

Escalation Transfer from assistant to human when a stop condition is met. Executed with a context packet and a two-sentence restart.

Exit criteria (pilot) Pre-agreed thresholds that determine scale/hold/stop: containment, CPR vs baseline, complaint/opt-out guardrails, disclosure %, incident-free days.

Explainability Clear, non-technical reasoning about what happened and why, suitable for customers and auditors.

Feature flag A switch to enable/disable features or intents instantly, supporting canary releases and rollback.

Friction Customer effort required to complete a task. Reduced by identity-once, pre-fill, relevant choices and honest pauses.

Golden answers Locked, versioned wording for regulated or risk-bearing statements that must not drift.

Guardrails Plain-English, versioned rulebook enforced by the assistant and recognised by humans: disclosure, identity, lawful basis/consent, do-not-automate, payments, language limits, rollback.

Hardship Customer circumstances indicating vulnerability or difficulty paying. Requires early escalation and minimum-facts capture.

Hindsight trail A readable audit of inputs, versions, tools called and decisions, enabling after-the-fact explanation.

Identity (verification) Establishing who the customer is, once, with the lightest method allowed, and carrying that status through the journey.

Incident An unplanned event impacting availability, confidentiality or integrity. Managed via detect → contain → communicate → recover →learn.

Intent The customer's goal, with a defined 'done' state in the system of record. Organises routing, knowledge and write-paths.

IVR (Interactive Voice Response) Menu-based telephony routing. A scale tactic that often traps nuance; not a substitute for outcomes.

KBA (Knowledge-Based Authentication) Identity checks that rely on personal trivia. Discouraged due to risk and poor experience.

Knowledge catalogue Versioned set of answers with owners and review dates; includes golden answers for regulated text.

Latency p50/p95 Time to first meaningful word or response at the 50th/95th percentile. p95 reveals peak pain customers feel.

Lawful basis Legal justification under UK GDPR for processing personal data (e.g., contract, legitimate interest, consent, legal obligation).

Legitimate interest (LI) Lawful basis where processing is necessary for a legitimate purpose balanced against individual rights. Requires a recorded balancing test.

Link (verified payment link) Secure, tokenised URL to a hosted payment page. The assistant issues and records link state; it never captures card data.

Logging (operational) Structured records of actions and versions for monitoring, troubleshooting and audit.

Microcopy Short service text that does practical work: disclosures, confirmations, choices with consequences, next steps.

Minimally viable inclusion Accessibility and language measures that ensure service works for people with different abilities, languages and bandwidth constraints.

MFA (Multi-Factor Authentication) Identity verification using two or more factors (something you know, have or are), typically required on admin consoles.

Observability Ability to understand what the system did and why through metrics, logs and traces. Reported via four views: experience, economics, quality & safety, reliability.

Opt-out A recorded choice to stop certain processing (e.g., marketing, automation). Must be honoured across channels.

Orchestrator The planning/execution component that builds short plans, calls tools, enforces guardrails and checks outcomes.

Outcome A change in the world verifiable in the system of record with a confirmation reference and timestamp.

PCI DSS (Payment Card Industry Data Security Standard) Rules for handling card data. This book's stance: never capture cards in channel; use links/hosted forms; log state, not numbers.

PECR (Privacy and Electronic Communications Regulations) UK rules covering electronic marketing and certain communications practices.

Persona (advisor) Human roles in service, focused on judgement, empathy, negotiation and finishing.

Pilot Time-boxed deployment to prove resolution, safety and economics under exit criteria.

Policy fence Deterministic rule enforced by the assistant before acting (e.g., change window, eligibility limits).

Privacy by design Embedding data protection into design choices: minimum necessary, identity once, short retention, transparency and auditability.

p95 budget Latency allowance at the 95th percentile for key steps. Drives caching, dependency contracts and escalation timing.

Redaction Removal of personal data from logs and analytics.

Redress Compensation or remedy granted during complaint handling. Usually reserved for human decision.

Resolution rate Share of interactions that reach the defined 'done' state. Not the same as containment.

Residency (data) Where data is stored/processed geographically. Often UK/EU for regulated contexts.

Reverse gear (rollback) Ability to revert a change safely and quickly. Rehearsed monthly.

Risk register Documented list of risks, mitigations and owners. Only useful when tied to controls and checks.

Rollback drill A scheduled rehearsal of turning off an intent or feature and recovering state.

RTT (Round-Trip Time) Network latency affecting perceived responsiveness. Managed with caching and edge decisions where justified.

Rulebook-first deployment Launching with guardrails, golden wording and reporting in place before full automation.

SLA (Service Level Agreement) Time commitments and quality thresholds (e.g., response time, resolution time) sometimes surfaced to customers.

Sensitivity (±10%) Range analysis on the two largest drivers (containment and escalated minutes) to show realistic financial outcomes.

Shadow mode 'Assistant' proposes actions; humans execute. Used to compare outcomes and harvest typed errors before going live.

Single sign-on (SSO) Central identity system allowing users to sign in once across multiple systems. Combined with MFA for admin surfaces.

Small plan A plan of at most three steps executed one at a time with checks in between. Reduces brittleness.

SoR (System of Record) The authoritative system where customer or transaction data is stored and verified.

Stop condition Explicit trigger to escalate: identity doubt, ambiguous intent/policy, missing write-path, distress language, customer requests a human.

Telemetry Operational signals used to run the service: metrics, logs, traces.

Timeout Exceeded time budget for a dependency or step. Triggers early escalation with context.

Tool (whitelisted) A named capability with input validation and post-conditions that reads/writes to systems of record.

Typed error Short, actionable failure class (e.g., identity_doubt, tool_timeout) owned by a person and retired or mitigated weekly.

Value per Resolution (VPR) Attributable uplift per successful resolution where relevant (saves, collections, upsell). Separate from CPR.

Versioning Assigning versions to guardrails, knowledge and releases so outcomes can be explained by date.

Verified identity state A carried flag indicating identity has been established to policy, including method and timestamp.

Verified link state The status of a payment link (issued, opened, paid, expired), stored instead of card data.

Write-path A safe, auditable way to commit a change in a system of record. Without a write-path, you cannot claim resolution.

Zero-data analytics Analytics approach that stores references and states rather than raw personal data. Helps minimisation and retention discipline.

More About the Authors

Keith Hamilton

Keith Hamilton is a UK commercial leader and AI strategist in the contact-centre industry. As Chief Commercial & AI Strategy Officer at Absolute Intelligence UK, he designs and scales blended human–AI operations for regulated and non-regulated sectors, with a focus on measurable outcomes.

Over a three-decade career spanning retail, e-commerce, technology services and healthcare, Keith has led revenue growth, customer operations and digital transformation in roles from supermarket manager to managing director and chief growth officer. His work has ranged from restructuring underperforming store estates to building out e-commerce and marketplace operations, and then into AI-enabled contact centres serving enterprise clients.

Keith's core discipline is operational economics. He thinks in baselines, intent volumes and unit economics: average handling time (AHT), first-contact resolution (FCR), customer satisfaction (CSAT), cost per resolution (CPR) and value per resolution (VPR). He is most comfortable when there is a clear before-and-after, a benefits tracker, named owners and a rollback plan that can be executed in hours rather than weeks.

keith@absoluteintelligenceuk.com

Lionel Thain

Lionel Thain is a British entrepreneur whose career has been shaped by data, consumer insight and the mechanics of scalable customer engagement. He founded Interactive Prospect Targeting PLC and MyOffers, pioneering large-scale consumer databases and running campaigns for global brands. At IPT, he also led a series of UK and international acquisitions that expanded the company's reach and cemented its leadership in performance marketing. IPT won a slew of awards from The Sunday Times (Tech Track 100), IDMF, Fast Growth Business Awards, and others.

In 2018, Lionel shifted his focus to the BPO sector, working closely with a 300-seat South African operation. Over the next five years, he played a strategic role in its transformation into the fastest-growing customer-service centre in the country, ultimately scaling to 4,500 seats in the Utility, Retail, Telco and Leisure sectors.

Lionel's philosophy is rooted in clarity as the engine of sustainable growth. He is particularly interested in how AI is reshaping the economics of service and how incentives can be aligned so that customers, agents and shareholders all benefit—while maintaining momentum without amplifying risk.

lionel@absoluteintelligenceuk.com

Together

Together, Keith and Lionel combine board-level commercial discipline with hands-on operational build. They approach AI in customer service as an operations and governance problem as much as a technology one: how to design journeys, roles, metrics and guardrails so that customers are better served, frontline teams are supported rather than undermined, and executives get outcomes they can measure and defend in the boardroom.

www.ingramcontent.com/pod-product-compliance
Lightning Source LLC
LaVergne TN
LVHW062124200926
848484LV00007B/1758
* 9 7 9 8 2 9 5 5 8 5 3 3 3 *